W9-AMP-048

# Containers
# for Patios

Chicago Public Library
Clearing Branch
6423 West 63rd Place
Chicago, Illinois 60638-5005

# Containers for Patios

Richard Rosenfeld

LONDON, NEW YORK, MUNICH,
MELBOURNE, DELHI

SENIOR EDITOR  Zia Allaway
SENIOR DESIGNERS  Rachael Smith,
Vanessa Hamilton
MANAGING EDITOR  Anna Kruger
MANAGING ART EDITOR  Alison Donovan
DTP DESIGNER  Louise Waller
PICTURE RESEARCH  Lucy Claxton,
Richard Dabb, Mel Watson
PRODUCTION CONTROLLER  Rebecca Short

PRODUCED FOR DORLING KINDERSLEY
Airedale Publishing Limited
CREATIVE DIRECTOR  Ruth Prentice
PRODUCTION MANAGER  Amanda Jensen

PHOTOGRAPHY  Mark Winwood

First American Edition, 2007
Published in the United States by
DK Publishing, 375 Hudson Street,
New York, NY 10014

07 08 09 10 11   10 9 8 7 6 5 4 3 2 1

Copyright © 2007 Dorling Kindersley Limited
Text copyright © 2007 Royal Horticultural Society

All rights reserved under International and Pan-American
Copyright Conventions. No part of this publication may be
reproduced, stored in a retrieval system, or transmitted
in any form or by any means, electronic, mechanical,
photocopying, recording or otherwise, without the prior
written permission of the copyright owner. Published in
Great Britain by Dorling Kindersley Limited.

A Cataloging-in-Publication record for this book is
available from the Library of Congress.

ISBN-13:  978-0-7566-1714-1
ISBN-10:  0-7566-1714-6

DK books are available at special discounts for bulk
purchases for sales promotions, premiums, fund-raising, or
educational use. For details, contact: DK Publishing Special
Markets, 375 Hudson Street, New York, NY 10014 or
SpecialSales@dk.com

Reproduced by Colourscan, Singapore
Printed and bound in Singapore by Star Standard

Discover more at
**www.dk.com**

R0411872668

# Contents

Chicago Public Library
Clearing Branch
6423 West 63rd Place
Chicago, Illinois 60638-5005

# Decorating with pots

One of the main attractions of container gardening is its versatility. You can plant almost anything in a pot and use almost any vessel as a container, to produce an infinite range of possibilities for your patio. Team topiary in a Versailles tub with elegant flowers in a simple color scheme for a formal arrangement, or go wild and select rustic containers filled with grasses and daisies to create a meadowlike effect. Whatever style you prefer, the exciting ideas in this chapter will provide a wealth of inspiration.

## Rustic and informal

Create a cottage-garden feel with terra-cotta, distressed-looking, or recycled containers. The more unusual, the better—anything goes, from rubber boots to buckets. Fill them with old-fashioned plants and flowers in lively colors.

*Pictures clockwise from left*

**Patio color**  Keep to an earthy theme with terra cotta and wood, and place the containers at varying heights. Use plants with striking foliage, such as ivies (*Hedera*), and primulas with their brash flowers in alternate pots for impact.

**Recycled glamor** You can use almost anything as a container, provided you can make drainage holes in the bottom. Kitchen rejects—an old saucepan and an olive can—make eye-catching pots for the contrasting show of blue campanulas and red-tipped sempervivums.

**Flower rowboat**  This shows how more or less anything makes a terrific container. Climbing annual nasturtiums (*Tropaeolum majus*) quickly dash over the sides in summer, giving a lively mix of fresh green leaves and orange and yellow flowers.

**Wickerwork**  Rustic baskets are ideal for primulas in punchy or pastel colors. You can fill a basket with several small pots, or one large one, or line it with bubble wrap with drainage slits in the bottom, before pouring in potting mix and planting it. A liner with drainage holes prevents damp soil from rotting the basket.

# Rustic and informal *continued*

*Pictures clockwise from left*

**Quirky shelving** One of the best ways of displaying ornamental pots is on a large, spruced-up, old bookcase or wooden shelving. This will need to be treated before being used in the garden, so that it does not disintegrate and rot in the rain. If you have a quirky space to fill, it is more sensible to hammer together your own customized display. Check that the shelving is sturdy because the pots become heavy after watering. A quick alternative is to arrange two or three treated planks of wood like steps on upturned clay pots or piles of bricks, with the lowest level at the front. When covered by pots, the foliage and flowers will hide the shelving and create an instant border that rises up in height.

**Splashes of red** A simple wood, stone, and gravel garden scheme is brought to life with hanging baskets and pots of pelargoniums. Lining up the pots on three sides frames the raised decking and dining area, giving it an instant visual lift. The bright red contrasts with the neutral background, and the exclusive use of one color adds a vital theme.

**A different angle** There are gaps in most garden borders that can be filled with old, chipped containers. Plant them with annual climbers, such as showy nasturtiums (*Tropaeolum majus*). Lying the pots on their sides injects extra informality, and sends the shoots every which way between shrubs and across paths. Alternatively, leave the pots empty and set them off by surrounding them with gravel topped with empty clam, oyster, and sea shells, and pieces of driftwood, or interesting items such as stained glass.

**Stacking boxes** Wooden crates or old storage containers can be piled up to provide instant height. Keep the look informal by arranging them none too neatly. Make the fuchsias bushier by pinching out their stem tips in spring. The new growth will quickly hide the soil and in summer there will be a lively show of flowers. You could even go one step further, training some of the plants at the edge to poke through the hand holes.

# Clean and contemporary

The modern look is a byword for sharp angular shapes and minimalism, using architectural plants, especially evergreens, to highlight the style. Geometry is in; overblown romantic gestures and clutter, out.

*Pictures clockwise from left*

**Blue horizons**  Neat upright planters, decorated in the same shade of blue as the background, bring color to this circular brick patio. They are planted with a tall, spiky, variegated cordyline, and a phormium behind. Note how the metal furniture adds an extra, shiny highlight.

**Scented corner**  Minimalism can quickly descend into sensory deprivation unless a range of scented plants is included. Metal pots with regal lilies (*Lilium regale*), all stout stems and strong presence, provide a richly scented midsummer show above a row of pots filled with lavender (*Lavandula*).

**Blocks of grass**  Eye-catching repeat planting works well with contemporary pots, such as these dark red acrylic blocks. Tactile, arching grasses spray out. Low-key planting around the bases of the pots doubles as a horticultural carpet, adding color and texture.

**Black and shiny**  The tall, black-stemmed bamboo *Phyllostachys nigra* is an excellent choice for a metal container. The new growth is dark green but turns shiny black within one or two seasons. Note how the colored mulch accentuates the color of the stems. When the stems become congested, repot in a larger container.

# Clean and contemporary *continued*

*Pictures clockwise from left*

**Greens and grays** Granite, metal, stone, and glass are cleverly combined in this contemporary sunken seating area. The bold design is complemented by rectangular windows and softened by the use of gravel-topped pots of sculptural foliage and oval-shaped, variegated hosta leaves in one corner. Note the use of a mound of foliage featuring a large fern in the other corner.

**Step by step** A wood and blue-metal pathway, complete with tiny spotlights, juxtaposes the natural and artificial. The raised beds are filled with plants of varying heights, including spiky irises and scented lavender, which work well against the backdrop of ladderlike verticals.

**Summer scents** Traditional cottage garden herbs, such as French lavender (*Lavandula stoechas*), have their place in a modern scheme, especially when planted in contemporary containers, such as this tall, ribbed pot. When selecting alternative herbs for large containers, make sure that they will provide plenty of growth and height: for example, sorrel (*Rumex acetosa*) grows to 4 ft (1.2 m) high, hyssop (*Hyssopus officinalis*), with its aromatic dark green leaves, grows to 32 in (80 cm) high, and sweet Cicely (*Myrrhis odorata*), which has small white flowers from spring to early summer, can reach a height of 3 ft (90 cm).

**Uniform look** Repeated planting lends itself to a huge range of styles, from the low-key to the strikingly upbeat. These lilies (*Lilium regale*) in black mesh pots stand out particularly well against the orange background and wood flooring.

# Formal elegance

Grand topiary shapes, mopheads, pyramids, spirals, and swagged pots create elegant lines and a cool, sophisticated look. Large, shaped plants are expensive, but boxwood can be quickly and cheaply styled into any design you want.

*Pictures clockwise from left*

**High standards**  A standard tree is one that has been trained to form a rounded head of branches at the top of a clear stem, like these large boxwood (*Buxus*) trees. While they are expensive to buy, they are ideal for adding evergreen structural interest, especially when used in pairs, as here, to frame a sculptural, eggplant-colored pot.

**Ivy swagging**  This mushroom-shaped honeysuckle (*Lonicera*) is a major focal point growing out of a lead tank, while its position at the window means that its scent will waft indoors. Small-leaved trailing ivy (*Hedera*) has been grown along a V-shaped stretch of chicken wire, and the whole scene is set off by neat balls of boxwood (*Buxus*) in pots.

**Theatrical patio**  Boxwood (*Buxus*) makes an excellent hedge, here neatly clipped and punctuated by mini pyramids as it leads into a patio. The seating area is framed by two flowering trees in pots, while the potted plant on the table behind fills the empty space.

**Baroque-style fernery**  An ornamental Italianate container filled with ferns highlights the low-key classical look of this damp, shady corner.

**Classical influence**  Identical potted plants create this cleverly structured scene. The outer spirals draw the eye to the peach-colored angels' trumpets (*Brugmansia*), which frame a classical statue and plinth. Reflective, ordered, and elegant.

# Formal elegance *continued*

*Pictures clockwise from left*

**Decked-out patio** The key ingredients of this mannered, set-piece scene are clean, straight lines, the orderly use of trees, and a concentrated burst of pastels. The planting is almost minimalist, with the bare-stemmed trees along one side of the decking given special prominence.

**Pillars of strength** The brick pillars of a modern conservatory become focal points when topped by urns filled with spiky succulents. Palms of varying heights soften the lines of the building, while summer flowers, including pelargoniums, lobelia, and marguerites (*Leucanthemum vulgare*), add color and impact on the ground.

**Classic urn** An Ali Baba pot takes center stage amid a soft, fluid, symmetrical scheme featuring soft grays and greens, and the purple of flowering chives (*Allium schoenoprasum*). A gravel path highlights the Edwardian theme.

**Pots, balls, and spirals** Evergreen topiary balls and spirals and sudden changes in perspective are packed into this small area, while the white pots provide a bright highlight.

# Mediterranean style

Private courtyards, framed views, terra-cotta tiles, olive oil jars, exotic leaves, and heady scents are hallmarks of the Mediterranean garden. Ideally, add a few drought-tolerant plants, some pelargoniums, herbs, and a lemon tree to complete the look.

*Pictures clockwise from left*

**Pots and tiles**  When containers look as good as these, forget about planting them, although you could insert a pot in the top and let a climbing nasturtium (*Tropaeolum majus*) or small-leaved ivy (*Hedera*) spiral out and down. When arranging pots to give antiquity and impact, opt for echoing shapes that build up in height, and either give them a prominent position or half-conceal them among arching ferns.

**Herb collection**  Colored tiles and a few old chunky pots give this collection of traditional herbs—mint (*Mentha*), fennel (*Foeniculum*), chives (*Allium schoenoprasum*), and parsley (*Petroselinum*)—a strong Mediterranean feel. Keep nipping back the herbs (not the fennel) for kitchen use and they will put out extra, bushier growth. Other essential herbs for the cook's garden include chervil (*Anthriscus cerefolium*), rosemary (*Rosmarinus officinalis*), thyme (*Thymus vulgaris*), basil (*Ocimum basilicum*), oregano (*Origanum vulgare*), and tarragon (*Artemisia abrotanum*).

**The view inside**  The large wooden doors, highlighted by an empty portly pot to the right, create a neatly framed view of the courtyard garden beyond. Note how the central row of reddish brown tiles leads the eye straight to the pots at the back. A similar framed view can easily be created for an Asian look. Use an ornamental window frame or make a large circular hole, to act as a picture frame, in a wall looking onto a courtyard. Then stand a large bonsai plant or Japanese maple (*Acer palmatum*) in a prominent position in the framed view.

# Hanging displays

Window boxes and hanging baskets are excellent for jazzing up dull or empty spaces. Give them a contrasting look every few months with seasonal plants, such as coral gem (*Lotus berthelotii*) and Italian bellflowers (*Campanula isophylla*).

*Pictures clockwise from left*

**Winter warmer**  A small plastic plant pot can easily be slipped into a wicker basket screwed to a wall. This simple winter scheme features pansies (*Viola*) at the front and pink and white heathers (*Calluna*) behind. Alternatively, try using variegated ivy (*Hedera*) with pink and green ornamental cabbages (*Brassica oleracea*). Primula, crocus, and dwarf narcissus provide spring color.

**Tiered effect**  Window boxes can be as spare and stylish or as outrageous and over-the-top as you want. This triple-layer scheme has dangling foliage at the bottom, with flashy begonias in the middle, and the tubelike flowers of a red fuchsia on top. Snip, snip, and snip again to keep the layers separate and all the flowers visible.

**Vibrant veranda**  Deep purple- and red-filled baskets provide great spheres of color, rhythmically and tastefully repeated around a white-painted veranda.

**Bursting with color**  A lively mix of pink petunias and yellow bidens creates an expanding, dangling ball of color. Use the biggest hanging basket available, plant densely, and keep pinching out the initial growth to encourage bushier plants and more flowers.

**Tray of flowers**  A wire tray on chains is a novel twist on a hanging basket and holds several pots of pansies (*Viola*) to add color to a fall or winter patio.

# Trees and shrubs

Container-grown trees and shrubs
are ideally suited to small gardens,
courtyards, or patios, and they can be
moved around as required. Use them
to frame doorways, or provide a focal
point. Choose small or dwarf varieties,
because fast-growing or large specimens
do not like being cooped up.

*Pictures clockwise from left*

**Fall color**  You need at least one tree or shrub for a
big burst of spring or fall color, and some, such as
amelanchiers, provide flashy displays at both times. Here,
a Japanese maple (*Acer japonicum*) adds rich reds and
yellows before leaf fall.

**Topiary with a twist**  An area of decking is given
a classical twist thanks to the boxwood (*Buxus*) topiary
corkscrewing up out of matching round pots, and well-
clipped boxwood balls at ground level. The scene can
easily be toned down or up by adding new topiary shapes,
from tennis rackets to aliens.

**Making an impact**  Four shiny, cylindrical planters are
filled with short standards of the Tasmanian cider gum,
(*Eucalyptus gunnii*), with its distinctive rounded blue-
green new leaves. Golden French marigolds (*Tagetes*)
planted at the base of each tree provide a striking contrast.

**Fun foliage**  Bay trees (*Laurus nobilis*) make excellent
container plants because they are slow-growing and
respond well to clipping. Here, a bay takes center stage
among potted ferns and an agave. The eye is drawn to
the different leaf shapes, showing that star performers
don't necessarily need to be frothy blasts of flowers.

# Container essentials

There are many different types and styles of containers, each producing a different effect; some suit formal schemes, while others are best for more naturalistic designs. In addition, the material your pot is made from affects its durability and cost. Antique stone containers, for example, are expensive, long-lasting, and very heavy, but you can buy cast-stone pots for less, while imitation plastic replicas achieve a similar effect for a fraction of the cost. This chapter explores the pros and cons of each type of container, helping you to make the best choices for your patio and your budget.

# Designing your patio

Think of your patio as a small garden and ask yourself two questions: what should you use instead of grass for the floor, and what can you use for the walls?

**Fixing the style**  Most design gurus agree that the look of a patio should be determined by the style of the house. So the patio of a period house needs paving or gravel and stone walls, while decking and trellis suit a modern home. The plants you choose—leafy and jungly, minimalist or colorful—also affect the look, so think before you buy.

**Beautiful backdrops**  Unless disguised by climbing evergreens, the walls will be prominent features of a patio, and need careful thought. Flick through a few garden design books for inspiration, looking at backdrops to see what's aesthetically and practically possible. Stuccoed walls in pastel shades (*below*) provide privacy, but if you want filtered views, trellis (*right*) is the best option. Trellis also has the added advantage of providing support for scrambling climbers and tomato plants.

**Decorative floors**  When the water from patio pots drains out, it can stain or rot lumber, which would be a shame if you have a beautiful deck. To prevent this, treat decking regularly with wood preservative, and remember that if your patio is in shade, it may become slippery in wet weather. Tiles, which come in a wide range of colors, may be a safer, more practical option. Or try pavers, which are extremely hardwearing. Whatever flooring you choose, drainage channels are essential. If you are using decking, create removable panels for clearing any blockages underneath.

Pavers are long lasting.

Treat wooden decks with preservative.

# Choosing containers

Before buying containers, work out what sizes you'll need, how they'll look, what plants you want to grow, and how much time you have for watering.

## Large containers

**Advantages** Large containers are instant focal points, so spend as much as you can on a few beautiful ones, and place them strategically. They don't need large plants—small plants look just as good—or you can leave them empty.

**Disadvantages** Large pots can be costly and heavy. They dominate small spaces, and may become superfluous if you restyle the garden regularly.

## Small containers

**Advantages** You can pack a huge number of small containers into a limited space, hanging them on walls and standing them on shelving supported by bricks at different heights, creating a traditional border with plenty of height at the back. Small, lightweight pots are also easily rearranged, and they can be squeezed into borders where gaps appear. There's a large choice available, from ornamental Italianate models to glazed pots in blue, red, or almost any color you like.

**Disadvantages** There are two main seasonal problems. In summer, the pots quickly dry out in hot weather, and may need watering three times a day. In winter, the roots are just the width of the thin pot away from icy winds and may freeze solid, so tender plants will need protecting.

# Wall pots and windowboxes

**Advantages**  Look in Mediterranean courtyards and you will see trailing pelargoniums, herbs, and other colorful plants in an incredible range of containers, nailed to the walls. They increase the scale of the garden, creating vertical planting space in small plots. Windowboxes also help to frame windows, and bring the garden up close to those inside the house.

**Disadvantages**  As with all small containers in full sun, they need frequent drinks in hot weather. When watered, the soil becomes surprisingly heavy, so wall pots and windowboxes must be fixed securely with nails or screws. Beware of water dripping down walls; marks may stain unless they are wiped away promptly.

# Hanging baskets

**Advantages**  You can squeeze a surprisingly large number of plants into hanging baskets, creating varied, layered displays with strong presence. The baskets can be subtle or magnificent, and used individually or in groups. The plants are also easily replaced each season for continuous, colorful displays. The baskets themselves can add fun anywhere from shoulder level to above head height, and there are many different types to choose from.

**Disadvantages**  Baskets need to be securely attached to the wall with brackets since they are heavy, especially when wet, and can cause damage or injury if they come crashing down. Check that no one is going to bump into them, and that they can be watered easily with a can or special hose extension.

# Creative combinations

A good way to decide on combinations of textures, colors, and shapes is to walk around a garden center, mixing and matching plants before you buy.

**Clever use of color**  Creating colorful combinations doesn't mean sticking exclusively to the bright and brash primaries with plenty of fizz. Try offsetting strong colors against quiet pale or dark tones. Orange stands out well against rich purples, especially here, where the long stems and flat, handlike leaves of the heucheras add texture and shape, too.

**Using texture**  Color gets a garden started, but the fine-tuning at the end needs to concentrate on foliage and contrasting textures: thick, fleshy, and upright, soft and floppy, rough and smooth. Choose containers that complement the plants. A pale glazed bowl sets off an *Agave americana* 'Variegata' (*below*) perfectly.

**Repeating themes**  For the best effects, repeated pots and plants need to be obvious, and an integral part of the design. Use large plants with lots of impact in bold containers or, if you prefer small plants, include multiple numbers and line them up where they can all be seen, creating a punchy effect.

# Balancing your display

All gardening is a glorified form of flower arranging; this is particularly true of potted displays, where you need to think about the look of the containers as well as the plants.

**Creating symmetry** Potted plants are incredibly versatile. Use them as stage props, helping to offset and/or highlight major features such as this wirework gazebo (*above*). The symmetrical pots embellish its bare legs, but you could go further and use climbing roses to cover the roof, and morning glory (*Ipomoea*) twined up the front two posts.

**Plants as sculpture** Try copying the Chinese and Japanese and use a few beautiful, shapely plants to create an eye-catching picture. The main subject here is the imposing bird of paradise flower (*Strelitzia reginae*), a South African perennial that needs a large pot. The wall color matches the foliage, and the orange flowers and a pair of shiny metal balls frame the scene, while the marble mulch complements the container.

**Rhythm and order** Repeat planting—and that applies to both containers *and* plants—has many advantages. It creates a formal, organized look, especially with topiary cubes and balls, and lends itself to echoes—here, the row of pots in the foreground is echoed by another row behind. Repeat planting can also propel the eye in a certain direction, either drawing attention to a display, or diverting the focus away from eyesores.

**Scale and proportion** Place a potted plant combination within a context, such as these two framing pillars. The pink masonry picks up the color of the osteospermums, while the container is large enough to take center stage. White gravel sets off the pastel theme.

# Choosing materials

Containers come in a wide range of materials, from metal to ceramic to wood, but the right choice for you depends on three key factors: the design of your garden or patio, where the containers are to be positioned, and the size of your budget.

An upbeat mix of styles, materials, and colors.

## Clay

**Advantages** Most garden centers now have a huge range of clay pots, from the tiny and inexpensive to wide-rimmed, big-bellied "sumo wrestlers" that can be very costly. Old pots (or reproductions) with swagged patterns add Renaissance antiquity and a sculptural touch.

**Disadvantages** Clay is porous and dries out quickly; a polythene liner can help reduce this problem. Also check that pots are frost-proof, not just frost-resistant. Make sure that plants aren't top-heavy, or the pot may blow over in high winds and break.

Clay pots are often best in semi-shade to prevent them from drying out too quickly.

## Wood

**Advantages** Solid hardwood barrels and containers made from logs are long-lasting and a good choice for permanent plantings in rustic settings. Large tubs have plenty of space for root development and extra plants—such as seasonal bulbs—around the sides.

**Disadvantages** Check whether softwood containers or windowboxes need treatment with a plant-friendly wood preservative. They also need to be lined with plastic to prevent soil from spilling out. Large barrels are heavy when planted, so plant them *in situ*.

Rustic wood is ideal for woodland plants.

## Stone

**Advantages**  Stone has a solid, antique look. Larger containers suit permanent plantings and offer plenty of room for root growth. Genuine old stone can be very expensive, but less costly modern copies in reconstituted stone or concrete are widely available. Smear with natural live yogurt to create an algae-covered surface.

**Disadvantages**  Since real stone is heavy, check its final position before planting. Large, expensive containers may need concreting in position to prevent theft. Gray stone can be dispiriting.

Soften a gray stone container with daisylike anthemis.

## Metal

**Advantages**  Shiny metal containers have great appeal, particularly in modern, minimalist settings. Use with shapely, sculptural plants, such as bamboos, grasses, and large-leaved exotics.

**Disadvantages**  Metal heats up quickly on scorching midsummer days. To avoid plant roots becoming frazzled in hot, quick-drying potting mix, line the insides of containers with bubble plastic or plastic sheeting. This will also act as a quilt in winter, protecting the roots from freezing temperatures.

Plant metal containers with spreading, shapely leaves for a sculptural touch.

## Synthetic

**Advantages**  A wide range of synthetic containers (usually plastic) are now available in many different colors and shapes. Inexpensive and fun in the right setting, they're also lightweight (for those with bad backs), and are ideal for roof gardens and balconies where you need to minimize the load.

**Disadvantages**  Not suitable for tall or top-heavy plants, which may blow over in strong winds. Avoid using them in sober, traditional settings, where they can look cheap and tacky.

Set off flashy containers with equally strong planting.

# Caring for your containers

All containers need thorough washing every so often to make sure they are clean and pest-free—but wood, metal, and stone pots may benefit from a little additional care to keep them looking their best.

**Protecting wood**  To prevent rotting, avoid exposing any part of a wooden container to wet soil. Treat wood before use by applying a wood preservative that isn't poisonous to plants, such as linseed oil (*left*). Repeat this treatment every year in winter, after you have cleaned out the container. Alternatively, protect wooden containers with wood stain that contains preservatives (*above*). Make sure the wood is clean and dry before applying the stain. Bear in mind the colors of your plants when choosing the paint color, to avoid alarming clashes. Quiet colors are invariably best because they blend with other pastels, and will set off brasher, bolder schemes. Finally, protect the inner surfaces of a container by lining it with plastic, ensuring that there are plenty of drainage holes in the bottom.

**Preventing metal from rusting**  Since galvanized steel won't rust, and stainless steel is unlikely to do so, rust isn't usually a problem. A metal watering can, left outside for several years, will still be rust-free. But if you need to drill extra drainage holes in a container that break through the protective seal, rust may set in. To prevent this happening, apply an anti-rust treatment around and inside the drilled holes, following the manufacturer's instructions. In general, try to avoid scratching metal containers, and keep them clean using any general-purpose nonabrasive household cleaner and a soft cloth.

**Aging stone containers** Modern or reproduction stone containers (or statues) often defeat their purpose by looking too clean, too bright, and too new when they're used to add instant antiquity. The quickest way to age a new stone pot is to promote the growth of algae by either smearing it with a mixture of cow manure and water, or painting it with natural live yogurt. You can also rub on some grass to encourage algae to grow. Some manufacturers of stone pots and ornaments make their own special aging solutions, which are quick and easy to apply.

**Preparing clay pots** If terra-cotta pots have been put in storage over winter, before you use them again give them a good scrub in warm water and detergent to get them scrupulously clean, and then hose them down. This helps eliminate the likelihood of pests or diseases affecting new plants. Also, clean the pots at the end of the season before you put them away. Before planting your pots, soak them in a bucket of water. This saturates the porous clay, which then draws less water out of the potting mix. Ornamental pots can be left out all year if they are frost-proof, but note that there is a difference between being frost-proof and frost-resistant: after a couple of winters outside, frost-resistant containers may start flaking and deteriorating. If in doubt, check with the manufacturer.

**Keeping synthetics clean** Like terra-cotta pots, synthetic containers should be cleaned and scrubbed in warm water and detergent before they are stored, and again when they are brought out for use. Stubborn stains can be removed with a kitchen scourer, but test a small, discreet area first to ensure that this will not scratch the pot. Choose a dark-colored container that won't show the dirt for permanent plantings that will sit outside all year.

# Planting containers

Before planting your containers, follow the tips in this chapter to make sure you select healthy plants. There is also advice on choosing the right soil to provide your plants with the best growing environment, as well as information on preparing pots for planting. Follow the step-by-step sequences for planting shrubs, climbers, summer pots, and hanging baskets to produce a patio overflowing with flowers and foliage. Hardy annuals are easy to sow from seed, too, and will create a sea of color in a sunny spot.

# Choosing healthy plants

When you have found the right plant, give it a quick once-over to make sure it is healthy. Remember that you're paying not only for what's above the soil, but also for a sturdy root system, and that needs to be checked along with the rest of the plant to make sure it will thrive.

**General tips**  As well as looking for plants with strong healthy growth, plenty of flower buds, and a thriving root system, make sure that they have a full spread of top-growth. Many plants have a "front" and "back" because nursery staff don't have time to keep turning them to the sun, and the growth may be lopsided. Avoid plants that have wilting or discolored foliage, as well as those with weeds growing out of the soil.

**Check the roots**  A good root system is like a well-maintained engine, and if an established plant doesn't have one, don't touch it. First, try to slide the plant out of the pot (not always that easy) and check that there's a good all-around spread of roots. Avoid pots where congested, restricted root growth means you can't see any soil, a problem known as "pot-bound," and/or when the roots curl out of the drainage holes and make a knotted clump. Being cramped like this invariably signals poor and sickly top growth.

**Reject plants with poor growth**  If an established plant has poor growth, there's a good reason for it. It may come from weak stock, in which case it will never amount to much, or it may have been badly neglected (*left*). The fact that it has been well watered on the day you see it doesn't exclude the possibility that it hadn't had a drink for days beforehand, or that it has previously been lying on its side in a shady corner. Fight the "I've-got-to-get-planting-this-second" bug, and don't buy until you've found a healthier, more vigorous specimen.

**Big isn't always best**  It's very tempting to buy the tallest or biggest plant available, but don't equate size with potential—that can be a waste of money. Look for a sturdy young plant with plenty of new shoots and buds as well as a healthy root system that will flourish (*right*), instead of one that's twice the size now but that is clearly going to end up spare, feeble, and gaunt. Give the former a good start, look after it well, and it will soon outperform the latter. This advice applies equally to climbers: the plant with the longest stems may end up producing the most vigorous growth, but equally, it may not. Instead of stem length, look for lots of healthy buds to avoid making an expensive mistake.

**Look for pests and diseases**  When buying from a reputable specialty nursery, it's very unlikely that you will encounter plant problems. At other outlets, unless you check that a plant has a clean bill of health, you risk buying an ailing specimen and spreading pests and diseases around your garden. Hold the plant up to the light and check both sides of the leaves and stems, particularly the new growth, looking for signs of pests (*see pp.114–115*). The best way to test for the presence of vine weevils in the soil is to give the stem a gentle pull. If the roots are being eaten, the plant will come away from the soil. Black deposits on the leaves indicate fungi growing on the excreta of sap-sucking insects, so check the plant for aphid infestation. Discolored leaves (*left*) may be the result of a nutrient deficiency or other ailment or disease.

# Choosing the right potting mix

There are four basic kinds of potting mix, but how do you know which one you need? Which is the best for long-lived plants? What's the fuss about peat? Are peat-free mixes any good? Here are the pros and cons.

## Loam-based potting mix

Also called soil-based potting mix, this is made from sterilized loam. It's often available in different recipes or strengths, ranging from formulations for seeds and cuttings to high-fertilizer formulations for long-term, large plants such as shrubs. Start fertilizing potted plants after three months, when the nutrients run out.

### Advantages

- *Different blends are formulated for different types of plants.*
- *Holds water well.*
- *Contains good supply of nutrients.*

### Disadvantages

- *Bags are heavy.*
- *Incorporates small quantities of peat.*
- *Variable quality. Check reviews of brands in the gardening press.*

## Peat-based potting mix

Also known as loamless or soilless potting mix, peat-based potting mix includes multipurpose types for seeds and general potting, and is best for short term, one-season displays. It is lightweight and well aerated, and the lack of nutrients is easily overcome by the use of slow-release fertilizers. When the peat dries out, it shrinks and can be difficult to rewet.

### Advantages

- *Easy to handle, being light and clean.*
- *Consistent, reliable quality.*

### Disadvantages

- *Dries out quickly.*
- *Prone to waterlogging.*
- *Low nutrient levels.*
- *Plants need fertilizing after four weeks (seeds) or six weeks (plants).*

Loam-based potting mix retains water and nutrients well.

Peat-based potting mix is the basis for many multipurpose mixes.

## Peat-free potting mix

As concern about peat-stripped areas and ruined habitats grows, so the sales of peat-free potting mix have increased. One of the best, and least environmentally damaging, options is green waste compost. Made from recycled household waste, it is dark, black, and heavy, and suitable for most garden and potted plant needs. Otherwise, try coir, or composted bark (except for use with seeds and seedlings).

## Coir-based potting mix

Made from shredded coconut husks, coir is sold either loose or in blocks; the latter need to be soaked for about 20 minutes before use. Since coir has no nutrients, it is generally mixed with multipurpose potting mix (one-third coir to two-thirds additional potting mix). Use it for annual displays in pots and containers where a lightweight potting mix is needed, such as windowboxes and wall pots, or on balconies. It dries out quickly and plants will need to be watered frequently.

**Advantages**

- *Good nutrient levels.*
- *Retains moisture well.*
- *Inexpensive.*
- *Heat treatment has eliminated pests, diseases, and weeds.*

**Disadvantages**

- *Some peat-free potting mixes give better results than others with certain plants.*

**Advantages**

- *Inexpensive.*
- *Lightweight.*

**Disadvantages**

- *Not entirely "green": peat-free, but it uses up thousands of air miles.*
- *Not for permanent displays.*
- *Plant performance can be variable.*

Peat-free potting mix is less harmful to the environment.

Coir-based potting mix is light, and useful for windowboxes.

# Preparing your pots for planting

All pots, large and small, need a few minutes' worth of preparation. Plants will live longer and look better if their pots are prepared well. Also consider the weight of your containers to avoid back-breaking lifting after planting.

**Check for drainage holes**  Most plant pots are made with drainage holes so that excess water can drain away (if it can't, plants will rot). If a pot doesn't have holes, you will need to make some. One way of doing this is to drill into the base several times with a masonry bit.

**Hammering holes**  You can either leave the drilled holes as they are, or tap them with a hammer to make one larger drainage hole. Choose clay containers with a thick base, which is less likely to fracture when hit with a hammer.

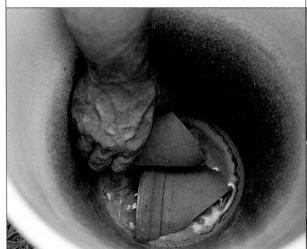

**Stop the rot**  To help water drain freely, place broken terra-cotta pots (crocks), polystyrene chips, or large pebbles in the base of the pot. Alternatively, use a layer of fine mesh with gravel on top. This prevents drainage holes from becoming blocked and soil from being flushed out.

**Lighten the load**  Any pot will be heavy when filled with soil, and even heavier after being watered. To reduce weight, fill the bottom third with polystyrene chunks or ceramic balls. Note that this applies only to pots for annuals or plants that don't have long, extensive roots.

**Reusing old pots** All pots, including those left in the garden or stacked up in the garage, must be cleaned immediately before use. This applies even if the pots were stored under cover and cleaned months ago, before being put away. Undisturbed pots can be breeding grounds for pests and diseases, larvae, and baby slugs. Don't risk it. Scrub scrupulously with detergent and rinse well. As an extra precaution, you can also soak pots in a mild bleach solution and then rinse well. This is advisable if the containers have previously housed diseased plants.

**Lining pots** Clay pots that have not been glazed on the inside are vulnerable to frost damage. This is because they are porous, and when water seeps into them and then expands as it turns to ice, the pot cracks. To prevent this, line pots that you want to sit outside all year with heavy-duty plastic. Always buy more plastic liner than you think you need. Push it well down into the pot, and use a pair of scissors to cut out drainage holes in the bottom. Then place a layer of pebbles or stones in the base, and fill up with potting mix, the weight of which will push the liner down further. Finally, trim away the excess liner flush with the top of the container. Lining terra-cotta pots in this way also prevents salts in the soil and water from leaching through the clay and discoloring your container.

**Moving heavy containers** It can be a nightmare trying to move large, filled, heavy pots unless you have help, and even then you are in danger of hurting your back and dropping the container. The best solution is to transport your containers on a sturdy wooden dolly, treated with wood preservative. To avoid lifting a filled pot, place it on the dolly before planting, and move to its final destination. The dolly can also double as a pot stand, eliminating the need to lift off the heavy container and allowing water to drain away efficiently.

# Container mulches

Choosing the right mulch is just as important as selecting the right plant or container. But with so many now on the market, how do you know which one best suits your needs?

**Tip for success**

In spring, after watering, scatter a thick layer of mulch evenly on the soil. Never compact or pile mulch up around the stem.

**What is mulch?**  Mulch is a layer of gravel or other material that helps lock moisture into the soil and reduces evaporation. It can also be decorative. Gritty mulches deter slugs and snails.

# Mulching options

**Chipped bark** Best used around shrubs and woodland plants, such as camellias, magnolias, palms, and rhododendrons. Ideal for wooden barrels. If there's a large, bare surface area, bark will help prevent weed seeds from germinating in the soil.

**Gravel** Available in different sizes and colors, gravel has a high aesthetic value, and guarantees efficient surface drainage. It helps to deter slugs and snails, and a thick layer will help retain moisture. Best for Mediterranean-style plants, alpines, and hostas.

**Pebbles** A large-scale version of gravel, also available in different sizes and colors, pebbles suit large seaside plants, and Asian-style and contemporary plantings in shiny metal containers. Best for bamboos, cordylines, grasses, and sedges.

**Seashells** Best for variety of shape, size, and color (from white to pink). Shells are ideal for grasses, lilyturf (*Ophiopogon*), and *Skimmia japonica* 'Rubella'. If shells are in limited supply, place them on top of a layer of pebbles.

**Crushed glass** This popular innovation, which is perfectly safe to handle, comes in various colors, and is ideal for modern schemes. Use with a sculptural plant, where nothing else detracts from the effect. Best for bamboos, dwarf palms, and yuccas.

**Recycled materials** Increasing numbers of recycled materials are coming onto the market, like computer screens scrunched into tiny colored pieces, or crushed shells (*above*), a waste product from the seafood industry. Best for modern schemes.

## Planting a shrub

Evergreen shrubs, such as hebes, make beautiful container features. For the maximum impact, buy a plant with healthy leaves and an attractive shape, and avoid those with lots of roots poking through the bases of their pots.

**1** First, check that the pot has drainage holes in the bottom, and drill a few if there are none. Place broken crocks, or pieces of polystyrene—old plant trays are ideal—on the bottom to aid drainage. Do not block the holes.

**2** Start filling the pot with fresh loam-based potting mix (avoid any with peat). If the soil is lumpy, break it up. Stop filling when you can stand the plant in its container on the soil with a 2-in (5-cm) gap to the rim of the pot.

**3** Place the shrub in its container in the center of the pot, and start filling around it, firming in the soil. The aim is to create a hole for the plant to slot into, in exactly the right place and at the right depth. If it's off-center, try again.

# Planting a shrub *continued*

**4** Gently lift the shrub in its container straight up and out of the pot, leaving the hole intact. If you haven't already done so, give the shrub a good drink and let the water drain away. This helps the plant get off to a good start.

**5** Carefully remove the shrub from its container, taking care not to damage its roots or break off any top-growth. Then tease out the roots at the edge of the root ball to encourage them to grow outward.

**6** Gently lower the shrub into the hole, and firm in the potting mix all around. Add a little more mix, if needed, to give a level surface, but make sure it is no higher up the stem than when the plant was in its original pot.

**7** Water in the shrub to settle the soil and to remove any air pockets. One good method is to pour the water onto an old crock so that it flows evenly and doesn't expose the roots. Repeat in each corner of the pot.

**8** As a final decorative touch, scatter gravel or small pebbles in a thin layer around the shrub. Available in various colors, they set off the plant and help to keep the potting mix moist by reducing evaporation.

# Planting a summer pot

Summer-flowering plants go on sale from late spring. Arrange them on the ground before buying, to ensure a lively mix of colors, shapes, and heights. Select plants that will flower all summer.

1   Instead of squashing a large number of shortish plants into a small container, go for a large, wide one. If it is deeper than you need, place an upturned pot in the center to save potting mix. Fill the gap with gravel or crocks.

2   Pour in the potting mix, then arrange the plants in their pots to check the display from all sides. Place those with trailing growth at the edge where the stems will spill over the rim, and the tall, upright ones in the center.

3   Soak all your plants before planting. Start in the center, working out to the rim. This ensures that you have enough space to plant your dominant plant without snapping off the stems and buds of the shorter ones around the edge.

4   Put in the outer plants, making sure they have room to spread. Finally, give the pot a good soaking with an upturned rose spray. Turn the pot daily so that the plants do not all lean one way toward the light.

# Make a hanging basket

Seasonal hanging baskets are easy to make, and can vary from the delicate and gentle to the big and blowzy. Plant the dominant plants on top and some decorative trailers around the sides.

1  Stand the hanging basket on a wide, short pot to keep it stable during preparation. Line the basket with a store-bought basket liner, or use sphagnum moss and pack it in tightly to a minimum thickness of 1¼ in (3 cm).

2  Lay a small circle of polythene over the liner at the base of the basket to help retain water. Cut out holes in the liner, about 2 in (5 cm) above the base, for your trailing plants. Fill the basket to that level with loam-based potting mix.

3  Wrap paper around the root ball of each trailing plant (like this ivy) to protect it, and gently insert through a hole. The roots should be level with the soil in the basket. Add extra potting mix and firm in.

4  Put a small plastic pot near the center of the basket to act as a watering reservoir. Plant short plants at the edge of the basket, and tall ones in the center. Fill in around them with potting mix. Water the plants through the plastic pot.

## Planting a climber

There is a lively choice of climbers for containers, which can be trained up a length of trellis, ideally against a backing fence or screen. Make sure there will be enough room for the plant to spread out.

**1** Choose a heavy, stable, frost-proof pot with drainage holes in the bottom. Add a layer of crocks around the base of the trellis to fix it in position and provide good drainage. Start adding loam-based potting mix.

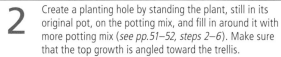

**2** Create a planting hole by standing the plant, still in its original pot, on the potting mix, and fill in around it with more potting mix (*see pp.51–52, steps 2–6*). Make sure that the top growth is angled toward the trellis.

**3** Fill in around the climber with potting mix, leaving a gap of 2 in (5 cm) from the soil to the rim of the pot. Tie in the stems loosely to the trellis with soft twine. When these stems have hardened, remove the ties and tie in new growth higher up.

**4** Water well with a watering can with an upturned spray, and add a layer of small pebbles or gravel over the surface to help highlight the display. Stand smaller potted plants at the front to create a mixed arrangement.

# Sowing annuals

The big advantage of growing brightly colored annuals is that you can try out new fun ideas and combinations each year. They are easily raised in spring, and keep impatient gardeners busy before the rest of the garden takes off.

**Tip for success**

Many small seeds need light to germinate. Perlite allows in light, and keeps them moist.

**1** Fill new or clean pots with seed-starting mix, adding some horticultural or sharp sand to improve drainage, and give them a quick tap to settle the mix. Make sure that there is a gap below the pot rim to allow for watering.

**2** Water the soil with warm water using an upturned spray. Hardy annuals can be left outside once sown, but half-hardy annuals need a warm, bright windowsill indoors, away from direct sunlight.

**3** Take a few seeds, and space them out on the soil. Cover them with sifted potting mix to the depth given on the seed packet. Really tiny seed is best mixed with fine sand before it is scattered over the soil.

**4** Clearly label each pot with the name of the seeds and the sowing date. This is particularly important when you do all your sowing on the same day. Place pots on a windowsill or in a greenhouse to germinate.

# Create a tower of climbing annuals

Some feature plants are best grown in pots where they are much easier to view and care for, and you can put them at center stage. These morning glories (*Ipomoea purpurea*) grow very quickly from seed sown in the spring.

**1** Arrange a wigwam of canes or old stems, such as stripped forsythia, around the edge of a container filled with potting mix. The wigwam doesn't need to be very neat—the stems will soon be obscured by the climbing plants.

**2** Tie the tops of the stems together. Then wrap string or raffia around the canes, about halfway up, to strengthen it. After planting, add more at different heights to make it easier for the climbers to spread across the frame.

**3** Make planting holes by each support with a trowel or spoon. Remove the seedlings carefully from their pots. Gently pry apart the plants, handling them by their leaves, not the delicate stems. Plant one in each hole.

**4** Firm all the plants in the soil, then water well. You may find it necessary to add an extra circle of twigs to help train the climbers onto the canes, and to stop them from climbing in the wrong direction.

# Container recipes

The most successful container displays marry beautiful plants with pots that show them off to best effect. The recipes in this chapter offer exciting combinations, while the symbols indicate the growing conditions that each plant prefers.

### *Key to plant symbols*

### Soil preference

| | |
|---|---|
| ◌ | Well-drained soil |
| ◑ | Moist soil |
| ● | Wet soil |

### Preference for sun or shade

| | |
|---|---|
| ☼ | Full sun |
| ◑ | Partial or dappled shade |
| ● | Full shade |

### Hardiness ratings

| | |
|---|---|
| ✳✳✳ | Fully hardy plants |
| ✳✳ | Plants that survive outside in mild regions or sheltered sites |
| ✳ | Plants that need protection from frost over winter |
| ✿ | Tender plants that do not tolerate any degree of frost |

# Spring scent

This elegant spring show builds up from the alternating white and blue hyacinths to the rich blue grape hyacinths (*Muscari*), hidden in their grasslike leaves, and up to the very beautiful Fuji cherry (*Prunus incisa* 'Kojo-no-mai'). The cherry carries its spring blossom on open, bare branches as the leaf buds are just about to break. When they do open, the bronze-red leaves are a big attraction for the first few weeks. They then green up over summer, turning orange-red in the fall before falling.

## Container basics

**Size**  Approx. 6-in- (15-cm-) diameter terra-cotta pots (hyacinths and grape hyacinths), and 18-in (45-cm-) diameter glazed ceramic bowl (Fuji cherry)

**Suits**  All gardens

**Potting mix**  Multipurpose potting mix

**Site**  Full sun

## Shopping list

- 8 x *Muscari neglectum*
- 3 x white *Hyacinthus orientalis*
- 1 x *Prunus incisa* 'Kojo-no-mai'
- 3 x blue *Hyacinthus orientalis*

## Planting and aftercare

Plant fresh hyacinth bulbs in fall, about 4 in (10 cm) from the top of the soil. Stand the pots in a sunny position sheltered from heavy rain, until the hyacinths flower in spring. Also in fall, plant the cherry and muscari bulbs, which should be set about 4 in (10 cm) below the soil surface. After flowering, the bulbs can be moved to a sunny bed with free-draining soil.

The cherry will reach 8 ft (2.5 m) high and wide in the open garden, and can be moved there when it gets too big for the pot. If you want to keep it miniaturized in a container, trim its roots each spring, and prune stems lightly in summer to keep its shape.

*Muscari neglectum*
❋❋❋ ◐ ◊ ☼

*Hyacinthus orientalis* (white)
❋❋❋ ◊ ☼

*Prunus incisa* 'Kojo-no-mai'
❋❋❋ ◐ ◊ ☼

*Hyacinthus orientalis* (blue)
❋❋❋ ◊ ☼

# Winter into spring

There are some excellent sweet-scented plants around at the start of spring, kicking off with the top-value 'Jetfire' daffodil (*Narcissus*), which grows to only about 8 in (20 cm) high. It is flashier than most daffodils, with bright yellow petals and a bright orange trumpet, and helps lift the dark green of *Skimmia* x *confusa* 'Kew Green', with its clusters of creamy-white flowers. This male skimmia can be used to fertilize a female, such as 'Isabella', which will then produce red berries. Underplant with a scattering of primroses (*Primula vulgaris*) to fill any gaps at the bottom of the display, and add a small-leaved trailing ivy, such as the 18-in- (45-cm-) long *Hedera helix* 'Jubilee', with its cream-edged leaves, to dangle over the side.

## Container basics

**Size** Approx. 18-in- (45-cm-) diameter, 24-in- (60-cm-) tall glazed ceramic pot
**Suits** Cottage gardens
**Potting mix** Multipurpose potting mix
**Site** Dappled shade

## Shopping list

- 5 x *Narcissus* 'Jetfire'
- 1 x *Skimmia* x *confusa* 'Kew Green'
- 2 x *Hedera helix* (variegated)
- 3 x *Primula vulgaris* (pale yellow)

## Planting and aftercare

In fall, plant the dominant skimmia first, then the primroses and ivy, inserting daffodil bulbs 4 in (10 cm) into the soil wherever you spot a gap. This display will need to be dismantled or moved into a larger pot when the skimmia gets too big; given a free root run, mature plants can exceed a height and spread of 9 ft (3 m). Alternatively, when it outgrows the pot, move it to the garden and replace with another young plant. Surplus daffodils can easily be pried out, and the ivy can be regularly nipped back to stop it getting out of hand.

*Narcissus* 'Jetfire'

*Skimmia* x *confusa* 'Kew Green'

*Hedera helix* (variegated)

*Primula vulgaris*

# Cool combination

A sharp arrangement with lean, arching top-growth and a downpouring of spreaders and trailers, all in green and white. The New Zealand cabbage palm (*Cordyline australis*) is the high point, with its stiff, arching, spiky leaves crowning the outward and dangling spread of the variegated spider plant (*Chlorophytum comosum* 'Variegatum'), the quick-spreading stems of the fleshy-leaved *Plectranthus madagascariensis*, and the bright white flowers of the busy Lizzie (*Impatiens* 'Accent White').

## Container basics

**Size**  Approx. 24-in- (60-cm-) diameter, 24-in- (60-cm-) high, white terrazzo pot

**Suits**  Contemporary gardens

**Potting mix**  Multipurpose potting mix

**Site**  Light shade

## Shopping list

- 2 x *Chlorophytum comosum* 'Variegatum'
- 1 x *Cordyline australis*
- 4 x *Plectranthus madagascariensis* or *Felicia amelloides* 'Read's White'
- 6 x *Impatiens* 'Accent White' or *Cuphea hyssopifolia* 'Alba'

## Planting and aftercare

The cordyline isn't completely hardy and will need to go in a sheltered spot over winter; if temperatures dive much below freezing, it should be brought indoors temporarily. The spider plant, which is typically grown on windowsills or in indoor hanging baskets, is even more tender. Although it will thrive outside over summer, it needs to be moved indoors for the rest of the year. The remaining plants are best grown as summer annuals, but the plectranthus—which needs a minimum temperature of 59°F (15°C)— can also be grown in a conservatory during the coldest months.

*Chlorophytum comosum* 'Variegatum'

*Cordyline australis*

*Plectranthus madagascariensis*

*Impatiens* 'Accent White'

# Bold and brassy

A fun scheme with bright, contrasting colors and rich scent that will fill front-of-patio gaps, giving a quick injection of maroon, yellow, and red. The container can also be used in front of a border where the planting has gone quiet, or even to help signpost the way to another part of the garden.

The chocolate cosmos (*Cosmos atrosanguineus*) provides the vertical interest, growing up to 24 in (60 cm) tall. It has silky petals and a rich scent of hot chocolate when standing in full sun. The twirly stems of the bidens scatter yellow flowers in all directions, and the pendula begonias help to hide the edge of the pot. The different leaf sizes—open, feathery greenery from the bidens and large triangular leaves from the begonias—add extra interest.

## Container basics

**Size** Approx. 18-in- (45-cm-) diameter, 12-in- (30-cm-) high, glazed ceramic pot

**Suits** Cottage gardens

**Potting mix** Multipurpose potting mix

**Site** Full sun

## Shopping list

- 3 x *Bidens ferulifolia* or *Tagetes* Gem Series
- 2 x *Cosmos atrosanguineus*
- 3 x *Begonia pendula*

## Planting and aftercare

Plant in spring or early summer, but do not put outside until after the last frost. When the summer flowering begins, keep deadheading to guarantee a continuous supply of flowers, and water and fertilize at regular intervals. The plants hate cold, wet winters, so bring them under cover in mid-fall. Cut off any dead growth, tidy up, and keep in a bright, frost-free place, watering just occasionally while dormant. Repot next spring with fresh potting mix.

*Bidens ferulifolia*
❄❄ 💧 💧 ☀

*Cosmos atrosanguineus*
❄❄ 💧 💧 ☀

*Begonia pendula*
❄ 💧 💧 🌤 ☀

## Alternative plant idea

*Tagetes* Gem Series
❄ 💧 ☀

# Summer spikes

A large, lively scheme that builds up in levels, from the cushions of blue lobelia up to the light blue salvia on stiffer, upright stems, and on to the higher, arching flashy orange-red crocosmia. These are all set against the bold, spiky cordyline, with its leaves like octopus tentacles rising up and over the pot. The mix of straight lines and informality at the base makes this display a good candidate for most situations, especially those demanding an eye-catching feature or focal point with plenty of presence.

The scheme kicks off in early summer with the lobelia, and is followed by the salvia, but it goes into overdrive when the crocosmia starts flowering in late summer. Crocosmias rarely feature in pot plant displays, which is a shame because they inject considerable impact.

## Container basics

**Size**  Approx. 18-in- (45-cm-) diameter, 18-in- (45-cm-) tall terra-cotta pot

**Suits**  Formal or informal situations

**Potting mix**  Multipurpose potting mix

**Site**  Full sun or light shade

## Shopping list

- 1 x *Cordyline australis* 'Sundance'
- 2 x *Crocosmia* 'Bressingham Blaze'
- 3 x *Salvia patens* 'Cambridge Blue'
- 4 x *Lobelia* (blue)

## Planting and aftercare

None of the plants pose any problems. The cordyline, salvia, and crocosmia are frost-hardy, which means the pot needs some protection over winter to avoid the prolonged freezing temperatures and heavy rain, while the annual lobelia can be discarded in winter and replaced in late spring. The crocosmia will need to be pried out (best done when repotting) every couple of years for permanent planting in a sheltered part of the garden, otherwise it will take over the scheme.

*Cordyline australis* 'Sundance'
❄❄ ◐ ◊ ☼ ◑

*Crocosmia* 'Bressingham Blaze'
❄❄ ◐ ◊ ☼ ◑

*Lobelia* (blue)
❄ ◐ ☼ ◑

*Salvia patens* 'Cambridge Blue'
❄❄ ◐ ◊ ☼ ◑

# Pastel pinks

This beautiful pastel arrangement has a gentle spread of evergreen, variegated, small-leaved ivy (*Hedera*) with pinkish stems overhanging the container, tiny clustered petals of the annual *Gypsophila* 'Gypsy Pink' above, and pink cosmos providing a focal point. What makes the scheme particularly appealing is the contrasting color and shape of the leaves: those of the cosmos are tightly packed, light, and feathery, while the ivy foliage is scattered and angular.

A low-key, stylish scheme like this is best given a prominent position, such as on a garden table, where it can be seen clearly and won't fade into the background—it is too good for that.

## Container basics

**Size**  Approx. 14-in- (35-cm-) diameter, 10-in- (25-cm-) tall glazed ceramic bowl

**Suits**  Informal and cottage gardens

**Potting mix**  Multipurpose potting mix

**Site**  Full sun

## Shopping list

- 2 x *Cosmos bipinnatus* 'Sonata Pink'
- 3 x *Gypsophila muralis* 'Gypsy Pink'
- 3 x *Hedera* (small-leaved, variegated) or *Helichrysum petiolare*

## Planting and aftercare

The only permanent ingredients in this scheme are the ivies or helichrysums— the annual cosmos and gypsophila are grown each year from seed and discarded at the end of summer. They can easily be replaced by late winter-flowering crocuses and/or *Cyclamen coum* to fill the gap before more pastels are planted the following spring. Then, as an alternative to the gypsophila, you can add the richly scented cherry pie (*Heliotropium*) in violet-blue. Over summer, keep deadheading to encourage more buds, and nip off any straggly ivy stems for neatness.

*Cosmos bipinnatus* 'Sonata Pink'
❄ ◐ ◌ ☼

*Gypsophila muralis* 'Gypsy Pink'
❄❄❄ ◌ ☼

*Hedera* (small-leaved, variegated)
❄❄❄ ◐ ◌ ☼ ☀

Alternative plant idea

*Helichrysum petiolare*
❄ ◌ ☼

# Tropical container

The best ingredients for a tropical pot have large, lush leaves (the banana plant, *Ensete ventricosum*); leaves with special shapes (*Melianthus major*) and colors (*Heuchera*); and extraordinary flowers (the spider flower, *Cleome*). This scheme, also includes a speckled-leaved calla lily (*Zantedeschia*) and, a complete surprise, wild rye (*Elymus*).

It is important that a tropical display doesn't look too contrived and neat. So plant the tall banana on one side, letting it dominate, with the contrasting bushy *Melianthus* beneath, and spiky *Elymus* centered in the foreground. Although the flowers are not the big attraction, make sure that the spider flowers are not masked by foliage and can be clearly seen.

## Container basics

**Size** Approx. 24 x 24 in (60 x 60 cm), 3-ft-(90-cm-) tall, brightly colored container

**Suits** Contemporary or tropical

**Potting mix** Multipurpose potting mix

**Site** Full sun

## Shopping list

- 1 x *Cleome hassleriana*
- 1 x *Ensete ventricosum*
- 1 x *Melianthus major*
- 1 x *Zantedeschia* 'Anneke'
- 1 x *Elymus magellanicus*
- 1 x *Heuchera* (purple-leaved)
- 3 x *Spilanthes oleracea*

## Planting and aftercare

Use a large, eye-catching, weighty pot that won't blow over. Stand it in a sheltered spot to stop the banana leaves from being flayed by winds. Water well over summer. The banana, arum lily, and *Melianthus* won't tolerate a cold, wet winter—though the *Melianthus* is hardier—and are best kept at 50°F (10°C) in a heated greenhouse. Discard the annual spider flower and *Spilanthes*, and grow them from seed the next spring.

Cleome hassleriana

Ensete ventricosum

Melianthus major

Zantedeschia 'Anneke'

Elymus magellanicus

Heuchera (purple-leaved)

# Silver shimmer

The extremely attractive purple evergreen leaves of *Heuchera* 'Stormy Seas' create the frame and setting for the shrubby, compact, silver-leaved evergreen *Convolvulus cneorum*. The silver is also picked up by the intricate patterning on the leaves of the cyclamen, which has exquisitely scented, long-petaled flowers in fall or early spring.

Eventually, the convolvulus and *Heuchera* will outgrow the pot—the smaller, less vigorous *H.* 'Can Can' might be a better choice in a restricted space.

## Container basics

**Size**  Approx. 12 x 12 in (30 x 30 cm), 24-in- (60-cm-) tall brushed metal container

**Suits**  Late summer to fall contemporary scheme

**Potting mix**  Multipurpose potting mix

**Site**  Bright light

## Shopping list

- 4 x *Cyclamen persicum* Miracle Series or *Primula* 'Wanda'
- 1 x large (or 2 x small) *Convolvulus cneorum*
- 4 x *Heuchera* 'Stormy Seas'

## Planting and aftercare

The cyclamen are tender, so place the pot in a heated greenhouse to protect from frost. When planting, the tops of the tubers should just poke through the top of the soil. When the leaves fade and plants become dormant, remove the tubers and keep them dry and warm until replanting in early fall. Or plant hardy cyclamen, such as *C. coum* or *C. hederifolium*, which can be left outside all year.

As the convolvulus grows, it can be either moved into a garden bed or given its own larger container with more colorful plants around the edges, including the dark-leaved *Heuchera*.

*Cyclamen persicum* Miracle Series

*Convolvulus cneorum*

*Heuchera* 'Stormy Seas'

### Alternative plant idea

*Primula* 'Wanda'

# Winter flower and foliage basket

The height in this basket is provided by the Mexican orange blossom (*Choisya ternata* Sundance), which forms the centerpiece. Its new foliage is bright yellow, compensating for the lack of flowers—it rarely blooms. The yellow contrasts with the dark green leaves of the spreading checkerberry or wintergreen (*Gaultheria procumbens*), which release a strong scent when crushed. The checkerberry has small white or pink summer flowers, followed by bright red fruits that last through the winter. Additional color comes from the violas, the white-centered yellow leaves of the *Lamium maculatum* 'Aureum', and the dark-leaved dangling growth of the ivy (*Hedera helix*).

## Container basics

**Size**  14-in- (35-cm-) diameter hanging basket
**Suits**  Formal or informal gardens
**Potting mix**  Multipurpose potting mix
**Site**  Dappled shade

## Shopping list

- 4 x *Lamium maculatum* 'Aureum' or *Euonymus fortunei* 'Emerald 'n' Gold'
- 3 x *Viola* (yellow)
- 2 x *Hedera helix* (dark-leaved)
- 1 x *Choisya ternata* Sundance
- 3 x *Gaultheria procumbens*

## Planting and aftercare

Deadhead the violas to promote a long-lasting display and a sharp contrast with the dark green ivy leaves. Tweak out the stems of the gaultheria so that the red berries can be clearly seen.

Eventually, the Mexican orange blossom will need more space. Although it can be planted out in the garden, it is probably better to discard it in favor of *C. ternata*, which has a ravishing scent and is a better garden plant. The lamium can also go into the border, where it makes excellent ground cover.

*Lamium maculatum* 'Aureum'
❄❄❄ ◗ ◌ ☼ ☀

*Viola* (yellow)
❄❄❄ ◗ ◌ ☼ ☀

*Hedera helix* (dark-leaved)
❄❄❄ ◗ ◌ ☼ ☀

*Choisya ternata* Sundance
❄❄❄ ◗ ◌ ☼ ☀

*Gaultheria procumbens*
❄❄ ◗ ☀

### Alternative plant idea

*Euonymus fortunei* 'Emerald 'n' Gold'
❄❄❄ ◗ ◌ ☼ ☼

# Winter glow

The yew (*Taxus baccata* 'Semperaurea') provides the highlight, making broad, bushy growth that holds on to its golden yellow color even in winter, provided it is given full sun. Expect an ultimate height of 30 in (75 cm); even though it can be cut back, its tendency to spread means it will eventually need a larger space. The thyme, which reaches 10 in (25 cm) high by 10 in (25 cm) wide, echoes the golden tints, while the ivy (*Hedera*) obscures the edge of the planter.

## Container basics

**Size**  24 x 12 in (60 x 30 cm), 9-in- (23-cm) tall wooden planter

**Suits**  Informal winter patio

**Potting mix**  Multipurpose potting mix

**Site**  Full sun

## Shopping list

- 2 x variegated ivy (*Hedera*)
- 3 x orange pansies (*Viola*)
- 3 x *Thymus pulegioides* 'Archer's Gold'
- 1 x *Taxus baccata* 'Semperaurea' or *Rosmarinus officinalis* 'Miss Jessopp's Upright'
- 2 x orange and purple violas (*Viola*)

## Planting and aftercare

Keep snipping back any straggly stems of yew to keep it dense and shapely, and to ensure that it doesn't obscure the other plants at the base. The ivy needs plenty of light, as does the thyme, which can be regularly snipped back and used for cooking. Deadhead the pansies and violas to encourage further flowering.

When the yew becomes too big, either replace it with a young version, grown from a cutting, or with the likes of *Rosmarinus officinalis* 'Miss Jessopp's Upright', a compact rosemary with a strong, upright shape, which grows slowly to achieve its ultimate height and spread of 4 ft (1.2 m).

*Hedera* (variegated)
❄❄❄ ◐ ◌ ☼ ◑

*Viola* (orange pansies)
❄❄❄ ◐ ◌ ☼ ◑

*Thymus pulegioides* 'Archer's Gold'
❄❄❄ ◌ ☼

*Taxus baccata* 'Semperaurea'
❄❄❄ ◐ ☼ ◑ ●

### Alternative plant idea

*Viola* (orange and purple violas)
❄❄❄ ◐ ◌ ☼ ◑

*Rosmarinus officinalis* 'Miss Jessopp's Upright' ❄❄ ◌ ☼

# Kitchen garden basket

It is easy to create a mini kitchen garden in a hanging basket. Use the largest basket available, and hang it where you can reach it easily. Plant the trailing cherry tomatoes around the edges. The best lettuces are the come-and-cut-again kind—you just snip off as many leaves as you need; red-leaved lettuces, such as 'Lollo Rossa', provide extra color. Add herbs such as sage (*Salvia officinalis*), and the French marigold *Tagetes* Gem Series 'Lemon Gem' for a flash of yellow.

## Container basics

**Size**  The biggest hanging basket available

**Suits**  A sunny spot near the kitchen

**Potting mix**  Multipurpose potting mix

**Site**  Full sun

## Shopping list

- 2 x trailing cherry tomato, such as 'Garden Pearl' or 'Tiny Tim'
- 1 x *Salvia officinalis* 'Icterina'
- 1 x red-leaved lettuce, such as 'Lollo Rossa'
- 1 x *Tagetes* Gem Series 'Lemon Gem'
- 1 x *Origanum vulgare*

## Planting and aftercare

Although you can buy the tomato and lettuce plants, you will get a better choice in a seed catalog. Sow the tomato seed in early spring indoors, and raise the seedlings on a windowsill before hardening off outside in late spring/early summer. Give a liquid tomato fertilizer once a week. The lettuce seed can be sown under cover in spring for planting out in early summer. Grow several different kinds of lettuce in succession so that the moment a gap appears, there is a substitute to fill it. The sage—available in all-green, variegated white and green, or green with pink, white, and purple ('Tricolor')—and oregano are best bought as young plants. When the sage gets too big, plant it out in the garden.

Tomato (trailing cherry)

*Salvia officinalis* 'Icterina'

Lettuce 'Lollo Rossa'

*Tagetes* Gem Series 'Lemon Gem'

# Creating a themed patio

Planting a pot or two for a patio is not very difficult, but creating a whole design scheme is more challenging. Here, a few themed patios show the components that are needed to produce a unified and effective planting scheme. You can either take inspiration from one design and follow the style closely, or use some of the elements, together with ideas of your own, to create a unique look. For some themes, like the tropical style, you will need particular plants to achieve the right effect, but for others, such as the recycled garden, feel free to adapt both planting and pots .

# Create a flower-filled summer patio

Choosing the right mix of plants for a summer patio is the easy part; the tricky part is organizing them to create the right overall look. In a small courtyard such as this, choose a mix of colorful summer annuals and leafy plants for a beautiful cottage garden effect.

**Pot clusters** (*right*) While deep borders often mimic team photographs, with the short plants at the front and the tall at the back, so that everything is clearly visible, some patios work better in terms of multiple groupings. Arrange the pots into a series of small groups of, say, five or seven, with each cluster offering height that is off-center, width, and interesting detail right at the front. The livelier the overall view, the more the eye moves up and down, and here and there, and the more you have to step forward to get a closer look, and then back to take it all in.
**Maximize planting** (*below*) In small, narrow patios, maximize the planting by using wall as well as floor space. Note the clever mix here of table pots, wall planters, and windowboxes, all of which add height and interest. Leafy plants, such as the *Fatsia* and hosta, provide a foil for the cottage garden-style flowers.

# Making a summer flower patio

Everything is in the details. You have bought the plants, lined them up, rearranged and tweaked them, but it's the special features—the novel touches—that make the ordinary "superb." And you don't need exotic or unusual plants to do it.

**Fill a fruit crate** (*right*) Plants can be given a huge visual lift by planting in an elegant, stylish pot or a big, fun container; likewise, collections of plants are boosted by clever groupings. This certainly applies to inexpensive annuals, such as the petunias, Swan River daisies (*Brachyscome*), and asters, shown here. Pot them up in inexpensive plastic pots and pack them into a fruit crate that has been given a lick of colorful weatherproof paint. Provided the plants are watered, fertilized, and deadheaded, they will flourish and by midsummer the pots will be hidden completely beneath a veil of flowers.

**Tumbling, dangling fuchsias** The best plants for covering an empty wall include bushy fuchsias with spreading, dangling stems that are weighted down when smothered in flowers. There is a huge choice of cultivars, including the white and purple 'Fiona' and the all-red 'Marinka'. Make sure that the flower colors stand out against the background.

**Dress up a trellis** Trellises are traditionally used to cover an entire wall, for tying in spreading climbers, and supporting plants with arching growth. But they can also be used in narrow, vertical spaces with pot plants fastened to them, as here. Make sure that the pots are securely attached, or fix them to the wall behind with screws, to cope with the weight of the soil after watering.

**Foliage foils**  When designing your summer-flowering patio, it pays to think hard about the shape, size, color, and texture of the foliage, as well as the flowers. Leaves play a key part because they act as a backdrop, a linking element and, in the case of evergreens, essential structure that stands out when the flowering plants are dormant or not in full bloom. Leafy plants to look for include the shapely and glossy, those with variegation, and the large and handlike. Also include plants that combine flowers with interesting foliage, such as begonias.

*Hosta*                    *Fatsia japonica*                    *Skimmia japonica*

**A cottage garden in pots**  The prime ingredients of a cottage garden include a fun, carefree design with plants merging into one another, plenty of scent, butterflies and bees, and a sea of summer color. Although cottage gardens have a relaxed feel, the most effective are carefully planned, so mixing up a batch of potted plants and letting them get on with it may simply not work. You must stay in control. Make sure that the spreading plants, such as lavender, are in their own pots where they will not overwhelm their neighbors. Check that the big attractions can be clearly seen, although they do not have to be in the foreground. Remember that there's no such thing as a "cottage garden plant," but the emphasis is decidedly on the old-fashioned, not the brand-new. Good choices for pots include daisy-type flowers, dahlias, campanulas, clarkia, and cosmos.

*Argyranthemum* (marguerite)          *Lavandula* (lavender)          *Clarkia amoena*

# A taste of the Mediterranean

The Mediterranean garden can be anything from stylishly chic and upbeat to unselfconsciously laid-back with an open, airy look. Inject a scattering of dominant plants to set the scene. Then move smaller pots around. Experiment. Play with different ideas.

**Stepping back** (*below*)  The key elements in this patio garden are the gravel, decking, paving, and wooden pergola, with each material creating a different platform for plants. The beachlike gravel is used for drought-tolerant grasses, which are perked up by the bright red pelargoniums. More ornamental plant combinations have been grouped on the neat decking. The open terrace is an ideal space for plants with large leaves, such as hostas and *Fatsia japonica*, and the pergola makes the perfect "peg" for hanging baskets and creates a sense of enclosure, echoing Mediterranean courtyards.

**The detail** (*right*)  This view of the same garden, taken from the paved patio adjacent to the house, shows how the mix of plants cleverly emphasizes leaf shapes, featuring arching and stiff verticals, dangling forms, and flat, rounded horizontals.

# Creating a Mediterranean patio

Finding brightly colored plants for a Mediterranean look is not a problem—garden centers are packed with them—but knowing which ones to choose and how to combine them can be tricky.

**Earthenware pots**  Terra cotta is the quintessential Mediterranean container. Visit the Minoan museum in Iraklion (Heraklion), Crete, and you'll see highly sophisticated and amazingly large Mediterranean pots, dating back to 1450 BC and beyond. Relatively cheap, modern swagged terra-cotta pots and the expensive, imported kind are now widely available, recreating the same look. Alternatively, you can easily opt for more basic models, provided they contribute a showy touch: a flash of pink busy Lizzies (*Impatiens*) works wonders. Failing that, try verbenas or petunias.

**Basket case**  Those with small Mediterranean courtyards and gardens utilize every inch by nailing containers to walls, letting trailing and dangling plants tumble, and projecting primary colors against white walls. You can easily copy the idea by hanging up interesting small wall containers (don't use large ones because they will become impractically heavy when wet) on fences.

**Structural props**  Inject drama into your designs by creating different levels, using raised beds and tall containers. The steps up to a raised level at the end of this garden also highlight the spread of pots, giving them a visual lift. The use of gravel makes an immediate contrast with the lighter-colored paving and accentuates the terra-cotta containers and colorful plants.

**Water features** Don't just concentrate on pots and structures: add a fun, water-filled container or a fountain. A large water feature in full sun, in a relatively bare setting, becomes an immediate "walk-over-and-dip-your-fingers-in" attraction. Alternatively, tuck one away among potted evergreens that provide mini hideaways and shade, and you might just acquire a resident frog. The range of suitable containers varies from wooden barrels to specially built, knee-high cast stone or concrete ponds decorated with ornamental tiles. Wall fountains add plenty of splash. You could opt for a solar fountain, which will send up a small jet of water, but it will not be as powerful or eye-catching as one powered by an electric pump. When choosing aquatic plants, check their eventual spread to avoid overcrowding.

**Color palette** Start by choosing your star plants, concentrating on those that provide a long show of color, and making sure you won't have bare summer periods. Go for the tried and tested, like pelargoniums, dahlias, and verbenas, and try out some of the many specially bred new selections. Pick these tender plants in the bright, hot colors seen in traditional Mediterranean courtyard gardens. Evergreens with shapely leaves are possibly more important than flowers because they keep the garden alive in winter. Place them strategically around the patio so that the eye moves from one to the next. Keep rearranging and trying out new combinations. The big advantage of pot-plant gardening is that everything is mobile; you don't have to dig anything up.

**Planting choices**

- *Chlorophytum*
- *Coreopsis*
- *Dahlia*
- *Geum*
- *Miscanthus*
- *Pelargonium*
- *Phormium*
- pink *Verbena*

| *Dahlia* | *Coreopsis* | *Pelargonium* 'Clorinda' |

# The tropical look

There is a huge range of widely available, often subtropical, large-leaved plants that can be grown easily outside in summer. In complete contrast to the archetypal English garden, flowers are out, and a great sweep of dramatic jungly leaf shapes is in.

**Tropical effects** (*right*)  If you have a sheltered courtyard or suburban garden with a gentle microclimate, you will have no trouble growing architectural tropical-style plants, although, come winter, the more tender types will need to be brought under cover. If winter storage is a problem, stick to hardier plants—the Chusan palm (*Trachycarpus fortunei*), for example, survives a few degrees below freezing, and can be left outside all year in mild areas with a little protection. The one thing you don't want is an open, windy site, because strong whippy gusts will batter and ruin the leaves, so create a shelter belt.

**Sun seeking** (*below*)  Choose the sunniest site for your tropical patio, and remember that this may not be the area closest to your house if your yard doesn't face south. Position sun-loving palms and succulents in the hottest spots, and shade-tolerant plants, such as hostas, beneath the canopies of the large-leaved exotics if necessary.

# Creating a tropical scheme

Tropical schemes are easily put together. Pick your star architectural plants, fill the gaps with flowers and foliage, then check that the pots and background create the right illusion. Simplicity is the key.

**Pots and backdrops** With the emphasis on bold, punchy, exotic planting, avoid pots that will upstage the plants. The latter should grab all the attention. Only try exciting shapes or painted pots where the plants command equal attention. Avoid anything green in the background (from decking to a lawn), so that all the leaves are clearly visible, without any competition.

**Permanent fillers** The choice of gap fillers is important because if all the plants are headline-grabbers, they will fight for attention, and you'll get more losers than winners. Use the fillers to guide the eye to the strongest shapes, and create breathing spaces. The most reliable and highly effective include shade-happy hostas and ferns.

- *Adiantum venustum*
- *Choisya ternata*
- *Dryopteris filix-mas*
- *Hebe*
- *Hosta* 'Blue Angel'
- *Hosta fortunei* var. *aureomarginata*
- *Hosta* 'Frances Williams'
- *Hosta* 'Halcyon'
- *Laurus nobilis*
- *Matteuccia struthiopteris*
- *Pieris*
- *Sasa palmata*
- *Sedum*

**Colourful accents** Tropical scenes demand sparing, judicious use of colour, just enough to hint at parrots and toucans. Traditional English bedding plants, such as petunias and busy Lizzies (*Impatiens*), are ideal, as are the flashier dahlias, red hot pokers (*Kniphofia*), ginger lilies (*Hedychium*), and montbretia (*Crocosmia*).

**Care tips for tender plants** Tender plants can be treated in four ways: grow them as annuals and discard at the end of the season; take cuttings from the parent (again discarded); keep the plants under cover over winter; or wrap the plant and pot in bubble plastic, or in straw inside a chicken-wire case.

# Tropical planting ideas

***Chamaerops humilis*** The slow-growing dwarf fan palm comes from southern Europe but is happy in colder areas. It makes a bushy, low-growing clump of stiff leaves, and is quite a rarity because it doesn't get ripped and ruined by fierce winds. Bring inside in winter in cold areas.

***Trachycarpus wagnerianus*** A slower-growing, neater version of the Chusan palm (*T. fortunei*), with smaller, straighter, stiffer, but equally splayed leaves. The extra rigidity and smallness mean it is better able to withstand windy sites. Move indoors in winter in cold areas.

***Agave*** These American succulents are all slow-growing. Tender *Agave americana* has extraordinary, long, saw-edged, viciously spine-tipped leaves, which can reach 1.5m (5ft) high. 'Variegata' has yellow-edged leaves but is more tender; and 'Mediopicta' has a yellow leaf band.

***Phormium cookianum* 'Sundowner'** One of the flashier forms of mountain flax, making a chunky clump with a burst of tall, arching, bronze-green leaves with pink margins. The summer flowers are a minor bonus, and are well worth leaving for the superb pods that follow.

***Musa basjoo*** The Japanese banana is hardy enough for mild inner city gardens. It puts on prodigious annual growth and has massive paddle-like leaves up to 1.8m (6ft) long. In cold areas, cut off the leaves when frosted, create a tube of chicken wire around the stem, and pack with straw.

***Canna* 'Striata'** With its 45cm (18in) high, vertical, paddle-shaped, green-and yellow-striped leaves, place this canna where the sun shines through it, to get the full effect. Orange, gladiolus-like flowers emerge above the foliage in midsummer. Bring under cover in winter.

# New ideas from old

Find inventive ways to keep the cost down and bolster the design of your garden by recycling. Mix old with new, but make the DIY element an important feature, and concentrate on the details as well as the big picture. More or less anything goes.

**Be creative** (*right*) In many ways, using recycled goods is more creative than blowing a fortune on designer items. All kinds of containers, from old boots and shoes to bathtubs, pots, woks, and kettles are likely contenders. If you really get the bug, go to a junkyard to find fun, quirky possibilities. You can even use an old jalopy of a two-seater sports car as a giant pot. Some containers, like the shoes, will last only one season, but no matter. All that counts is that the plants grow well, they can be easily watered, and the water can drain out freely.

**Plant ladder** (*below*) Stepladders make useful shelving units. Balance small pots filled with dangling flowers on the treads from top to bottom. Place the ladder in a sheltered position to protect it from being blown over, and keep the DIY theme going with more recycled containers on the walls and ground.

# Recycling ideas for a patio

So many objects can be recycled that it is easy to create particular themes. You can keep to a simple, cottage-garden style, go for a Mexican theme with hot colors, or experiment with an Asian look. Invariably, you will need only a couple of authentic pieces to create the right atmosphere.

**Imaginative ideas** Old bathtubs or large containers are exactly right for bushy shrubs like lavender (*Lavandula*) (*right*), and for plants that spread and clump up. They are particularly useful when the garden soil is heavy clay and you want to grow plants that need light, free-draining soil, such as pinks (*Dianthus*). When the plants are richly scented, it is a good idea to position the container near seating. Just make sure that your recycled container has a few drainage holes in the bottom.

**In proportion** The scale of the flowers and the kettle, and the color combination, make this a good feature for the front of a display. You can choose the most exciting recycled container and the most gorgeous plant, but if they don't complement each other, think again.

**Hanging cups** A trio of enameled camping cups, bound together, hang from a beam. Since it is difficult to add drainage holes to the cups, place the plants still in their pots in the cups. After watering, remove the pots so that excess water can drain away.

# Plants for tiny cups and containers

There is a wide choice of plants for small pots, ranging from alpines and annuals to succulents. Check the eventual height and spread but, if in doubt, visit a garden center with your proposed container, checking for the best combinations. Either go for a mix of plants or choose several of the same kind in different colors. Verbenas come in reds, white, purples, and blues; violas and busy Lizzies are available in an equally rich mix.

**Plants to choose from**

- *Bellis*
- cacti
- *Dionaea muscipula* (Venus fly trap)
- *Drosera* (sundew)
- *Impatiens*
- *Nemesia*
- *Pelargonium*
- *Petunia*
- *Sempervivum*
- *Verbena*
- *Viola*

*Impatiens*            *Verbena* 'Sissinghurst'            *Viola*            *Sempervivum*

**Display stands**  Once you have checked out obvious pot stands, such as old bookcases and pallets (*above*), try resale shops and rummage sales for anything that will look the part (probably with a lick of exterior or wood paint), and go for sturdy, wide structures.

**Wild water features**  Keep the inventive, idiosyncratic DIY theme going, using old rubber tires for a fountain. A hose is inserted up a vertical length of pipe, topped by an upturned copper bowl with a hole in the top. The water splays out, across, and down the tires.

# Caring for containers

Plants in containers need regular care to keep them strong and healthy. Unlike those in the ground that can search the surrounding soil for moisture and nutrients, plants in pots rely on you to supply the essentials. In this chapter, explore ways to keep soils moist and plants well fed, and learn about the pests and diseases that may threaten your displays. In addition, discover how to keep tender plants warm through winter, and how to repot plants that need a new, bigger home.

# Watering your containers

Potted plants depend on you for all their needs, and since they can dry out within hours in summer, giving them a life-saving drink is a top priority. Here are some effective watering methods to save you time and minimize waste.

**Boosting moisture levels** Mix water-retaining gels with soil (following the manufacturer's instructions), and spread evenly. The gels absorb water and swell to many times their own weight, releasing moisture to plants over several seasons. Plants that benefit most from such gels are those that grow rapidly and are planted in light soil, from which moisture quickly evaporates.

**When to water** Potted plants need watering all year round, except in freezing conditions. In winter, the rain may do it for you, but keep checking because foliage can act like an umbrella, or a wall can create a dry spot. Water in the early morning or evening when evaporation rates are lowest. Use a rain barrel to collect rainwater for watering mature potted plants; use tap water for seedlings and young plants.

**How to water** The best way to water is with a watering can with a fine spray, which distributes water evenly and so won't compact the soil. If you don't have such a can, place a piece of slate or old crock into the corner of a pot, tilted downward, and gently pour water onto it. This method also prevents soil compaction and gives an even distribution of water. Repeat in each corner.

**Keeping baskets moist** In hot summer winds, hanging baskets dry out more quickly than most containers. Use water-retaining gels (*see opposite page*) to help counter this, and invest in a special extension hose so that you don't have to hold up hefty watering cans and can target the soil in your baskets more easily.

**Automatic watering systems** These are expensive and can be a little tricky to install, but they are very effective, water-efficient, and particularly useful when you go on vacation. You set the times when the system starts and stops, and determine how much water is needed. All you need is an outside faucet and an adjacent area where plants can be lined up. If you're away for a long time, ask someone to check that the system is working properly.

**Rescuing dried-out pots** If the soil in the pot has shrunk, add a few drops of dishwashing liquid to the water in your can to help re-wet it. For badly wilted plants, stand the dried-out container in a bowl of water and place it in the shade for about 30 minutes; then remove from the bowl. If the plant has collapsed, submerge the pot in a bucket of water until no more air bubbles escape, then remove and leave it in the shade until next morning.

# Fertilizing container plants

For most of its life, a container plant will depend on you to fertilize it in the growing season to ensure a good supply of flowers and strong growth.

**Before you plant** It's worth noting that a potting mix's nutrient content will be washed out and used up after six weeks in the case of soilless mix, and after eight to ten weeks with the soil-based kind. Thereafter, fertilize at fixed intervals, or add a slow-release fertilizer. These small round pellets (like tiny eggs) are added to the potting mix in the spring. Lasting about a season, they absorb moisture and release it with the fertilizer.

**When and how to fertilize**
Plants need a balanced supply of nutrients to grow, flower, and develop a strong root system, but this boost can be given only when they are actively growing. It is also crucial to follow the manufacturer's instructions. Overfertilizing won't produce bigger, stronger plants—in fact, a surge of excess chemicals can be incredibly damaging. If you are not using slow-release pellets (or similar treatments), try a fertilizer that comes in liquid or powdered form (to be dissolved) that is applied on watering. The main foods are nitrogen (N), which promotes good top growth, phosphorous (P) for healthy roots, and potassium (K) for abundant fruit and flowers. The relative amounts are usually shown on the packet—for example, "NPK 6:4:4."

**Food for flowers and fruit** A regular high-potash (potassium) fertilizer is essential when growing the likes of tomatoes and dahlias, and plants in hanging baskets, for a good crop of fruit and flower buds (it's even good at ripening wood). It is usually applied from the moment the first buds appear, but don't use it too early in the season, when it's essential that the plant builds up a good, all-around structure with plenty of new shoot and root growth.

**Leaf boosters** Most plants initially benefit from a balanced fertilizer to build them up, before a fertilizer aimed at specific needs is applied. A high-nitrogen fertilizer boosts leaf growth, and some plants, such as bougainvillea, benefit from this before being given a high-potash fertilizer to promote extra flowers. Plants grown for their foliage, such as hostas (*below*) and coleus (*Solenostemon*), need a nitrogen fertilizer in summer to promote a terrific display of leaves.

**Fertilizing lime-haters** Some plants, such as azaleas, camellias (*below*), kalmias, and rhododendrons, hate alkaline conditions and need to be grown in a special acidic (ericaceous) potting mix. Widely available, ericaceous potting mix has a pH of 6.5 or less (the pH denotes the degree of acidity or alkalinity in the potting mix). Such plants are usually clearly labeled. When watering, ideally use rainwater or, if that's impossible, cold, boiled water.

**Permanent container plants**
Every other year at the start of the growing season (depending on the rate of growth), permanent container plants will need rejuvenating, or they quickly decline. This involves potting them on, top-dressing, or repotting. Potting on means moving the plant up to a larger container with new potting mix to provide more room for root growth. With top-dressing, the top inch (2.5 cm) of potting mix is removed and replaced with a new layer. Repotting means taking the plant out of its pot, shaking off old soil, teasing out the roots, and adding new potting mix before putting the plant back in the same pot.

# Deadheading and pruning container plants

To make sure that flowering plants continue to bloom for the longest possible period, and to keep shrubs and climbers healthy, prolific, and in good shape, you need two techniques: deadheading and pruning. Both are quick, simple, and highly effective.

**Deadheading** Snipping off fading or dead flowers is an essential way to keep plants looking good. It ensures that drab old flowers don't detract from the new—there's nothing worse than fading white flowers turning an unsightly brown. Removing them also means that plants don't pour their energy into producing seed, which is the principal aim of a flower. Instead, the plants' energy is channeled into making more, high-quality flowers for a long display.

**Why prune?** Many shrubs and climbers need pruning to keep them vigorous and shapely and their flowers clearly displayed, and to stop their growth from becoming a tangled mess. Pruning is also essential because it eliminates weak, damaged, diseased, and dead growth, so that plants put all their energy into growing strong, healthy stems. When pruning it's important to know what happens next. Usually new growth shoots out from below the cut. A hard prune generally results in a mass of new vigorous growth, while a light pruning gives more limited results. Check your plants' needs before acting.

**When to prune** New deciduous shrubs should be pruned when dormant in winter, or after planting, to build up an attractive framework. Prune trees in winter, too, except *Prunus* species, which are pruned in summer. Established deciduous shrubs that flower in spring on stems made the previous year should be pruned after flowering. Shrubs that flower in summer on the current year's stems are generally pruned in early spring. Deciduous climbers are pruned likewise, depending on when they flower, and evergreens are pruned in mid- to late spring. Always use clean, sharp tools and wear protective gloves.

Prune shrubs with opposite pairs of buds with a straight cut.

For alternate buds, use an angled cut just above a bud.

Remove stems that are rubbing others, causing abrasions.

Cut all dead and dying wood back to healthy growth.

**Pruning deciduous shrubs and climbers** Make a downward-angled cut about ¼ in (5 mm) above a strong bud, with the base of the cut on the opposite side to the bud so water drains away from it. Try to cut above a bud pointing in the required direction. Where buds are opposite each other, make a straight cut above them.

- *Bougainvillea*
- *Clematis*
- *Hydrangea serrata*
- *Weigela*
- *Wisteria*

The pruning cut on this clematis is just above a new shoot. Take care not to damage it.

Prune mophead hydrangeas in spring, taking flowered stems down to healthy buds.

**Pruning evergreens** Cut out any dead or unproductive stems right back to the base or to green shoots. Do not prune into old, brown lavender stems because they will not reshoot. Give a light all-over trim to regulate the shape. Remove any dead flowers.

- *Berberis*
- *Elaeagnus pungens*
- *Euonymus fortunei*
- *Gaultheria mucronata*
- *Mahonia*
- *Pieris*
- *Viburnum davidii*

Carefully remove any dead growth in spring before the new growth develops.

This mahonia's long, dominant stem is being cut back in spring to produce a better shape.

**Trimming back trailers** Trailers look most effective when they produce a bushy mass of long growth. To keep growth dense, regularly nip back the stem tips in the growing season to force buds lower down to shoot out. If a plant has become quite "leggy," with just a few lengthy, dangling stems, pinch or cut these back in spring to activate more buds lower down.

- *Campanula isophylla*
- *Helichrysum petiolare*
- *Lobelia erinus*
- *Tropaeolum*

Nip back the long flowering stems of shrubby, silver-leaved *Helichrysum petiolare*.

Regular trimming in spring and summer helps the plant produce more trailing stems.

# Problems with pests

Humans can't avoid getting ill, and plants can't escape pests and diseases. Fortunately, most can be countered or minimized by organic or inorganic means and, except in rare cases, the garden will continue to look amazing.

**Preventing attacks** Selective biological control involves watering pathogenic nematodes (microscopic animals) into potting mix, when it is at a certain temperature, to kill vine weevils and slugs (don't use in conjunction with chemical controls). Other biological controls are available for red spider mite, whitefly, and aphids.

**Taking early action** Regularly examine a plant's soft new growth where sap-sucking pests are most likely to congregate. They're easily missed if you don't check the undersides of leaves. If you spot a few aphids, squash them between your fingers before they cause problems. Beetles, slugs, and caterpillars can be picked off.

**Chemical controls** Use chemicals only when really necessary (not for minor infestations at the end of summer, for example). Select the appropriate product, follow the manufacturer's instructions, store safely, keep away from children, never mix with other chemicals, and use in the early evening or morning on windless days.

**Encouraging friendly predators** Rather than using chemicals, which can enter and poison the food chain, create sites for wildlife, such as ladybugs, frogs, and birds, which eat slugs, aphids, and other undesirables. Infestations won't be wiped out instantly, as with chemicals, but you should notice the effects in the long term.

# Identifying common pests

**Thrips** Also called thunderflies, these tiny, black, narrow sap-sucking insects strike in hot, dry conditions causing silver-whitish mottling.

**Vine weevils** Fat, whitish, legless subsoil larvae with brown heads that eat a plant's roots, causing death. The adults are black beetles.

**Leaf miners** The mine—the white or brown dried-up part of the leaf—is caused by larvae of flies. They attack chrysanthemums and related plants.

**Red spider mites** Minuscule spider mites (reddish in winter) appear in warm, dry conditions, under the leaves, which turn yellowish white.

**Lily beetles** Easy-to-spot bright red beetles with black heads, found on lilies and fritillaries. It is a recent arrival from Europe.

**Caterpillars** The larvae of moths and butterflies. Most caterpillars feed on leaves, but some attack stems and roots as well.

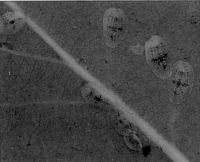

**Scale insects** Tiny brown or grayish white, sap-feeding insects, found on foliage and stems. Some excrete a sticky honeydew.

**Aphids** Small sap-sucking insects that multiply rapidly, stunting growth. Act quickly because they reproduce at an alarming rate.

**Slugs and snails** Inescapable, slimy, night-feeding mollusks that chomp through soft new stems, flowers, and leaves, and destroy seedlings.

# Preventing diseases

Even though healthy plants resist problems better than weak ones grown in poor conditions, they're not immune to diseases. Here's a quick guide to the symptoms, and the best solutions.

**Act quickly** It's usually impossible to spot the offending fungi (though some are just visible), viruses, and bacteria, but their symptoms are invariably obvious. In all cases, take prompt action, such as spraying, and cutting away and destroying the affected growth, and the problem should be relatively easy to minimize and control.

**Tackling diseases** Fungal and bacterial infections are spread mainly by spores, facilitated by moisture on the leaves or in the soil. Keeping infections out is impossible, especially when spores are spread by wind, but you can minimize their effect—for example, by promptly removing leaves and stems attacked by powdery mildew before it puffs out more spores. If you're growing roses, choose disease-resistant varieties. Where conditions are such that a rose regularly gets black spot, either grow something else (in severe cases) or spray it with an appropriate fungicide every week or two from early spring onward as a prevention. When spraying, always wear gloves or wash your hands thoroughly afterward. Sterilize pruners after using them on diseased plants.

**Detecting viruses** Viruses can be a major setback, reducing vigor and growth, and invariably producing discoloration. They are often spread by sap-sucking insects, one very good reason to create natural habitats for birds, ladybugs (which hibernate in hollow stems), and other natural aphid predators. You can also grow plants like marigolds that attract parasitic wasps, which feed on aphids. If you decide to spray the aphids, it may kill their predators, giving the next generation of these pests a free run. Wait and see if the predators tackle the problem before spraying. Group 9 Rembrandt tulips are particularly prone to a virus that produces "broken" flowers with wonderfully attractive white and feathered markings (*right*), but it can also be transmitted to other tulips.

# Identifying common diseases

**Rust** Small bright orange or dark brown blistering on the leaf or stems, with affected areas withering and possibly dying, caused by fungi in damp conditions. Rarely a major problem; remove affected areas and spray with an appropriate fungicide.

**Rose black spot** Evident in warm, moist conditions, producing black spots on leaves, then yellowing and leaf fall. Some roses are more susceptible than others; tackle by repeat-spraying and/or pruning from spring, and destroy the fallen leaves.

**Powdery mildew** White powdery spores and yellowing usually appears on upper leaves initially, caused by fungi encouraged by dry conditions. Treat by watering regularly, pruning affected areas and promptly destroying infected parts, and spraying.

**Rhododendron bud blast** Flower buds covered by tiny black fungi fail to open and turn brown, possibly hanging on for years, though not all buds may be affected. Spread by leafhoppers in midsummer. The only action is to remove affected buds.

**Sooty mold** Usually black (sometimes green) mold caused by fungal growth on the honeydew excreted by sap-sucking insects, which may actually be active on the higher leaves of an adjacent plant. Control by removing the insects, where possible.

**Gray mold (botrytis)** A common fungus producing fluffy grayish white mold on decaying and dead tissue. Remove and destroy affected parts. Prevent by improving air circulation, avoiding overcrowding, and removing fallen debris.

# Protecting pots over winter

Tender plants will die if their roots are locked in cold, wet soil in winter and temperatures dive well below freezing, but it takes just a few minutes to protect them in fall.

**Bring tender plants inside**  Bring plants that need a frost-free minimum winter temperature into a mildly heated greenhouse or conservatory, or cool room in your home, before bad weather sets in. Water occasionally.

**Wrap up delicate pots** Many pots, especially ornamental containers that aren't designed to stand outside in freezing temperatures, need winter protection. Wrap them up in burlap (possibly double layers), and secure tightly at the top and bottom with strong garden string.

**Keep tender plants warm** Wrap potted plants that need protection in low temperatures in layers of horticultural fleece before freezing weather strikes. Move the pot to a sheltered spot, such as a shed, away from flaying winds. Remove the fleece when the weather improves.

**Line clay pots** Insert bubble wrap inside clay pots in spring to minimize moisture evaporation, and to help keep the roots snug in winter when the temperatures dive—the roots are just a fraction of an inch away from the icy cold, unlike those deep down in the soil.

**Plants to protect** As a general guide, exotic plants from warm climates need winter protection. Some may survive the cold but, because they come from areas with dry winters, they will die in sopping wet soil. In free-draining soil and a sheltered position, though, they may survive. Others need to be wrapped up and brought inside, but the degree of protection varies.

**Plants needing winter protection**

- *Abutilon megapotamicum*
- *Aeonium*
- *Aloe vera*
- *Beaucarnea recurvata*
- *Begonia*
- *Bougainvillea*
- *Brugmansia*
- cactus
- *Citrus*
- *Echeveria*

- *Fuchsia* 'Thalia'
- *Helichrysum petiolare*
- *Heliotropium*
- *Jasminum polyanthum*
- *Lantana camara*
- *Livistona chinensis*
- *Musa*
- *Nerium oleander*
- *Pelargonium*
- *Tibouchina*

*Brugmansia suaveolens* yellow-flowered          *Lantana camara*          *Pelargonium*

# Repotting an overgrown shrub

All permanent shrubs need repotting into a bigger container, usually every two years in spring. This gives the roots more space to grow and an energizing "meal" of fresh potting mix.

**1** Lay the pot on its side, ask someone to hold it, and gently ease out the plant by pulling its stem. If you're in danger of damaging the plant, or it is stuck, slide a long kitchen knife around the insides of the pot to free the root ball.

**2** The roots will probably be in a tightly congested lump, in which case use a hand fork to pry out the encircling growth, and shake off the old "dead" soil and surface moss. Aim to create an open spread of roots.

**3** Cut back the main thick anchoring roots by up to one-third, but leave the thin, fibrous roots unpruned. Pruning promotes the growth of more thin roots, which absorb moisture and nutrients.

**4** Replace the old crocks in the base of the new, bigger pot, pour in some potting mix, and position the plant. Once the plant is centered and upright, pour in more potting mix, firming it down, and water in well. Top off with gravel.

# Plant guide

The following plants are all suitable for patio containers, and have been grouped according to their height and sun requirements.

## *Key to plant symbols*

### Soil preference

| | |
|---|---|
| ◊ | Well-drained soil |
| ◖ | Moist soil |
| ● | Wet soil |

### Preference for sun or shade

| | |
|---|---|
| ☼ | Full sun |
| ◑ | Partial or dappled shade |
| ● | Full shade |

### Hardiness ratings

| | |
|---|---|
| ✳✳✳ | Fully hardy plants |
| ✳✳ | Plants that survive outside in mild regions or sheltered sites |
| ✳ | Plants that need protection from frost over winter |
| ⌂ | Tender plants that do not tolerate any degree of frost |

# Tall plants for sun (Ab–Co)

### Abutilon 'Nabob'

With maplelike evergreen leaves and lax stems, 'Nabob' has a long summer show of rich crimson flowers. Provide a stout cane to keep it vertical, and water well in summer, with a monthly liquid fertilizer. Water less in winter and bring indoors. Prune lightly in spring.

**H**: 6 ft (1.8 m), **S**: 6 ft (1.8 m)
❁ ◐ ◌ ☼

### Agave americana

A sculptural succulent with a rosette of tough, pointed, spine-tipped leaves, yellow-edged in 'Marginata'. Grow in cactus mix. Water well in summer, giving occasional liquid fertilizer, but keep dry in winter, when it also needs to be kept under cover.

**H**: 4 ft (1.2 m), **S**: 4 ft (1.2 m)
❀ ◌ ☼

### Akebia quinata

The climbing chocolate vine gets its name from the small, dark purple spring flowers which have a vanilla scent on warm days. Stand against a sunny, sheltered wall and train stems against wires. Prune gently in early spring if necessary.

**H**: 6 ft (1.8 m)
❁❁ ◐ ◌ ☼

### Azalea

There are two kinds of azaleas: larger azaleas for outdoors and small indoor hybrids. Of outdoor varieties, 30 in (75 cm) high 'Rose Bud' has rose pink flowers in spring; taller 'Freya' has late spring orange flowers. Both need ericaceous soil and a sheltered site.

**H**: to 4½ ft (1.3 m), **S**: to 4½ ft (1.3 m)
❁❁❁ ◐ ◌ ☼

### Bougainvillea 'Scarlett O'Hara'

A flashy red Mediterranean climber that can be used as a border filler or focal point on a patio. Its side-shoots need cutting back in fall, leaving three to four buds. Water freely in summer, with a high-nitrogen fertilizer. Bring indoors in winter.

**H**: to 6 ft (2 m)
❁ ◐ ◌ ☼

### Brugmansia suaveolens

This brugmansia has long, tubular, white or yellow flowers, their scent strongest in early evening. The large leaves are a feature, but they are easily flayed by the wind, which is why all angels' trumpets need a sheltered position.

**H**: 6 ft (1.8 m), **S**: 6 ft (1.8 m)
❀ ◐ ◌ ☼

### Brugmansia suaveolens
*yellow-flowered*
A superb, tall plant, best grown as a multistemmed standard, with huge tropical leaves and scented yellow flowers. Stand in a sheltered, sunny position and bring indoors in mid-fall. Prune in early spring.

**H**: 6 ft (1.8 m), **S**: 6 ft (1.8 m)
❀ ◊ ◊ ☼

### Choisya ternata
Mexican orange blossom is a fine evergreen for late spring with richly scented white flowers. The crushed leaves smell peppery. Shear all over after flowering to encourage a second, smaller burst of flowers. Can be pruned quite hard for shape.

**H**: 4 ft (1.2 m), **S**: 4 ft (1.2 m)
❀❀❀ ◊ ☼

### Citrus limon *x meyeri* '*Meyer*'
Lemon trees (actually shrubs) are easily grown in pots to stand outside in summer. With ample summer watering and fertilizing, they produce fruits, which take 6–9 months to ripen. Lemons need a conservatory with some humidity in winter.

**H**: 6 ft (1.8 m) **S**: 4 ft (1.2 m)
❀ ◊ ◊ ☼

### Clematis '*Doctor Ruppel*'
A deciduous climber with large, 8-in-(20-cm-) wide, deep rose pink flowers with darker bands. They appear in early summer, with a second burst in late summer. Prune in early spring by about half the stem's length. Train new growth up a trellis.

**H**: 6 ft (1.8 m)
❀❀❀ ◊ ◊ ◐ ☼

### Clematis macropetala
This deciduous climber is one of the earliest flowering clematis, and has small, bell-shaped, blue flowers from late spring. Excellent cultivars include deep blue 'Lagoon' and lavender-blue 'Maidwell Hall'. All like a sheltered, sunny position, and some support.

**H**: 6 ft (2 m)
❀❀❀ ◊ ◊ ◐ ☼

### Cobaea scandens
A fast-sprinting annual climber, the cup-and-saucer plant produces fleshy, bell-like flowers that turn creamy green to purple. Provide trellis or taut wall wires for it to cling to, and keep other showy plants away from it, or they will be smothered.

**H**: 11 ft (3.6 m)
❀ ◊ ◊ ☼

# Tall plants for sun (Co–La)

### Cordyline australis
Slow-growing New Zealand cabbage palms have excellent forms for tubs. The long, pointed leaves of Purpurea Group offer light bronze hues to dark shades of purple; 'Torbay Dazzler' has cream stripes and edging. Water moderately in summer, less in winter.

**H**: to 4 ft (1.2 m), **S**: to 4 ft (1.2 m)
❄❄ ◊ ◊ ☼

### Crocosmia
Hardly a typical potted plant, but it can be used in large containers for a few years before being thinned or moved to a garden bed. Bright red 'Lucifer' is one of the best; late-summer 'Star of the East' is orange. If clumps get congested, lift and divide in spring.

**H**: 3 ft (1 m), **S**: 3 in (8 cm)
❄❄ ◊ ◊ ☼

### Eccremocarpus scaber
The Chilean glory flower is a tropical evergreen climber that produces masses of growth and bunches of flashy orange-red flowers. They start opening at the end of spring and continue into fall. Wall supports are essential, as are sun and shelter.

**H**: 10 ft (3 m), **S**: 10 ft (3 m)
❄❄ ◊ ◊ ☼

### Elaeagnus pungens 'Frederici'
One of the best evergreens for a pot, this compact, slow-growing shrub has bright yellow leaves edged in dark green. It has sweetly scented, whitish fall flowers and red fruit after a hot summer. 'Maculata' has more striking, yellowish leaves.

**H**: to 10 ft (3 m), **S**: to 10 ft (3 m)
❄❄❄ ◊ ◊ ☼

### Fatsia japonica
Evergreen Japanese aralia adds a strong presence to a shady corner. Grown for its mass of large, shapely, deeply cut shiny leaves; creamy white flowers appear in fall. If it gets too big, cut back the main stem in spring; new shoots soon appear.

**H**: 6 ft (1.8 m) or more, **S**: 6 ft (1.8 m)
❄❄ ◊ ◊ ☼ ☼

### Ficus carica
Common fig has a punchy presence with its large, lobed leaves. Use a pot 15–24 in (38–60 cm) wide and deep; stand in a sunny, sheltered place. In summer, water well and fertilize weekly. Initially, prune branches by half in spring for a productive framework.

**H**: to 8 ft (2.5 m), **S**: to 8 ft (2.5 m)
❄❄❄ ◊ ◊ ☼

### Hebe '*Great Orme*'

The evergreen hebes make excellent container plants. This is a compact shrub with bright pink flower spikes, gradually fading to white, from midsummer to mid-fall. It has shiny green leaves and dark purple shoots. Prune gently in spring to tidy up.

**H**: 3 ft (1 m), **S**: 3 ft (1 m)
❄❄ ◐ ◌ ☼ ☀

### Humulus lupulus '*Aureus*'

Golden hop is a fast-climbing perennial producing a superb mass of large, yellow-green leaves from spring to fall, providing a bright contrast to other climbers. Grow up a sunny trellis or wall wires. Use the flowers in dried displays.

**H**: to 12 ft (4 m)
❄❄❄ ◐ ◌ ☼

### Ipomoea '*Grandpa Otts*'

Climbing morning glories come in many colors, this annual being an intense, rich purple. Plants can be left to twine up and around a tall wigwam of canes, other climbers or even shrubs. It is easily grown from seed in spring. Shade from fierce sun.

**H**: 6 ft (1.8 m)
❀ ◐ ◌ ☼

### Jasminum officinale

The rampant, climbing, white-flowered jasmine has an intense summer scent, best appreciated in a sheltered spot. Young plants twirl around canes but mature plants in large tubs need wall wires. Prune quite hard in spring if needed.

**H**: 9 ft (2.7 m)
❄❄ ◐ ◌ ☼

### Juniperus communis '*Compressa*'

Ideal if you need a slow-growing, slender, upright, bright green conifer. Makes an excellent feature in a large trough with alpines or contrasting, smaller, rounded conifers; it requires minimum care. 'Brynhyfryd Gold' has a golden tint on new spring foliage.

**H**: to 1.6 ft (2 m), **S**: 12 in (30 cm)
❄❄❄ ◐ ◌ ☼ ◐

### Lantana camara

An evergreen shrub with clusters of bright flowers, ranging in color from white to yellow (aging to red), orange, pink, red, and purple. It makes a good standard. Grow against a wall in summer, and bring indoors in winter.

**H**: to 4 ft (1.2 m), **S**: to 4 ft (1.2 m)
❀ ◐ ◌ ☼

# Tall plants for sun (La–Pa)

### Lathyrus odoratus
Annual climbing sweet peas come in a wide color range; the best have a powerful scent. Grow from seed in fall or early spring; at 3 in (8 cm) tall, pinch out stem tips for bushier growth. Grow up a wigwam of canes with a wrap-around of string.

**H**: 6 ft (2 m)

❄❄ ◐ ◊ ☼

### Laurus nobilis
Bay trees are often best grown as standards with a ball of aromatic evergreen leaves on top of a bare stem 3 ft (90 cm) or so tall. Provide a sheltered, sunny position. Clip for shape in summer.

**H**: to 6 ft (1.8 m), **S**: to 18 in (45 cm) as a standard

❄❄ ◐ ◊ ☼ ☼

### Lilium *Citronella Group*
This nearly head-high lily is ideal for large pots because its bright lemon yellow speckled summer flowers stand out like exotic, hovering butterflies. They contrast well poking above and between the shapely leaves of cordylines and melianthus.

**H**: 4½ ft (1.3 m)

❄❄❄ ◐ ◊ ☼

### Lilium regale
This lily gives sensational results in midsummer, with large, purple-backed white flower trumpets and a strong, sweet scent ('Album' is all-white). Plant bulbs in fall at a depth of about 8 in (20 cm) and 4–8 in (10–20 cm) apart.

**H**: 4 ft (1.2 m), **S**: 36 in (90 cm)

❄❄❄ ◐ ◊ ☼ ☼

### Livistona chinensis
The Chinese fan palm has shiny, rounded leaves divided into long, thin fingers on a stiff, upright trunk. It is a slow grower, putting on only a couple of leaves a year. In theory, it can reach a huge size, but in a pot, it does not usually exceed 36 in (90 cm) high.

**H**: 36 in (90 cm), **S**: 18 in (45 cm)

❀ ◐ ◊ ☼

### Lobelia cardinalis
A twin-purpose summer perennial that excels in a container display (it must not dry out), and in an aquatic basket at the edge of a pond. It has dark reddish purple stems, bronzy leaves, and scarlet flowers. Keep in damp soil indoors over winter.

**H**: 4 ft (1.2 m), **S**: 36 in (90 cm)

❄❄❄ ◐ ◊ ☼ ☼

## Melianthus major

One of the best architectural plants, the shrubby honeybush has large, toothed, gray-green leaves. Provide sun and shelter; the latter is crucial in winter, when the top-growth dies back. If severe frosts threaten, throw some protection over the container.

**H**: 4 ft (1.2 m), **S**: 4 ft (1.2 m)
❄ ◊ ☼

## Myrtus communis *subsp.* tarentina

Ideal against a wall in a sheltered spot, myrtle is a bushy Mediterranean shrub with evergreen leaves, aromatic when crushed. Tiny white berries follow pinkish white late summer flowers. Avoid cold, windy sites. Give a spring trim, if required.

**H**: 4 ft (1.2 m), **S**: 24 in (60 cm)
❄❄ ◐ ◊ ☼

## Nerium oleander

Mediterranean rose bay is grown for its flowers and leaves. Typically pink flowers ('Casablanca' offers white; 'Ruby Lace', red) appear over a long summer period; leathery leaves are thin and pointed. Water sparingly in winter; prune for shape in late winter.

**H**: 6 ft (2 m), **S**: 3 ft (1 m)
🏵 ◊ ◊ ☼

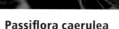

## Nolina recurvata

The bottle palm is an evergreen with a swollen base set in the soil, a short main trunk, and a wild topping of long, thin leaves. Use pots a size or two too small, and water only when the top of the soil has dried out. Water less in winter and bring indoors.

**H**: 6 ft (1.8 m), **S**: 4 ft (1.2 m)
🏵 ◊ ☼

## Olea europaea

Olive tree with tiny yellow flowers that needs a chilly winter and a long hot summer for a crop of olives. Water with care in summer, giving a liquid fertilizer monthly; water sparingly in winter. The self-fertile 'Aglandau' is the hardiest.

**H**: to 10 ft (3 m), **S**: to 6 ft (2 m)
❄❄ ◊ ☼

## Passiflora caerulea

The blue passion flower is a vigorous evergreen climber with startling flowers mixing white petals, a black ring, blue frills, and a prominent green stalk. Outside, provide a sunny, sheltered spot and give the stems a trellis or wired wall/fence to climb up.

**H**: 9 ft (2.7 m)
❄❄ ◊ ◊ ☼

# Tall plants for sun (Ph–Yu)

### Phormium tenax
Perennial New Zealand flax makes a clump of spiky, swordlike leaves, with long spikes of dull red flowers in summer. Brash 'Dazzler' has bronze leaves striped pink, red, and orange; 'Variegatum' is edged creamy yellow. Give it a sheltered spot over winter.

**H**: to 6 ft (2 m), **S**: to 3 ft (1 m)
❄❄ ◐ ◊ ☼

### Rhodochiton atrosanguineus
An unusual, easily grown climber. From summer to fall it has pink-purple, parachute-like flowers with a long, protruding, maroon tube. Being tender, it is grown as an annual outdoors; train it up a wigwam of canes in a pot or against wall wires.

**H**: 6 ft (1.8 m)
❀ ◐ ◊ ☼

### Rosa 'Golden Showers'
A remarkably free-flowering climber, with sweet-scented flowers (good for cutting) that turn from bright yellow to lemon and cream. They invariably appear in small clusters, and stand up well to heavy rain. One of the most successful roses against a north wall.

**H**: 8 ft (2.5 m)
❄❄❄ ◐ ◊ ☼

### Rosa 'L. D. Braithwaite'
A gorgeous, bright red bushy rose, with loose, free-and-easy growth. The fully open flowers are scented only when they are about to peak. Prune in late winter by half to two-thirds; lighter pruning gives more summer stems with smaller blooms.

**H**: 3½ ft (1.1 m), **S**: 3½ ft (1.1 m)
❄❄❄ ◐ ◊ ☼

### Rosmarinus officinalis 'Miss Jessop's Upright'
This rosemary has a strong, upright shape, valuable in winter when gardens are quiet. Thin the growth when cutting for cooking to prevent it from becoming a bushy blob. Light blue flowers appear in mid-spring.

**H**: 4 ft (1.2 m), **S**: 4 ft (1.2 m)
❄❄ ◊ ☼

### Salvia guaranitica
An ideal candidate for an ambitious display needing a tall vertical with dark blue flowers. It needs protection over winter (cut stems back to soil level). Water liberally over summer and give a monthly fertilizer, but water sparingly in winter.

**H**: 4 ft (1.2 m), **S**: 24 in (60 cm)
❄ ◐ ◊ ☼

### Sarcococca confusa

Christmas box is the ideal shrub for midwinter because of its scented white flowers, followed by tiny black berries. Extremely tough, it can easily be placed in a shady spot. If sited in full sun, keep the soil moist. Spring prune to keep it shapely.

**H**: to 4 ft (1.2 m), **S**: 30 in (75 cm)
❄❄❄ ◐ ◌ ☼

### Sollya heterophylla

The evergreen Australian bluebell creeper has thin, twining woody stems and sprays of pale blue flowers all summer followed by cylindrical seed pods. Stand in a conservatory or frost-free greenhouse from fall to early summer. Pink forms available.

**H**: 4 ft (1.2 m)
❄ ◐ ◌ ◑

### Tomatoes

The fruit comes in pink, purple, yellow, and orange as well as red, and is easily grown from seed. Tie upright cordons to sturdy canes. Nip off the main stem after four or five flower clusters, remove sideshoots, and fertilize regularly; water liberally.

**H**: to 6 ft (1.8 m)
🏠◐ ◌ ☼

### Trachelospermum jasminoides

The evergreen star climber has a lovely, delicate scent and needs to romp up wall wires or an adjacent, sturdy climber. The glossy green leaves turn reddish bronze in winter. Put it in a warm spot. If growth is too much, cut back after flowering.

**H**: 13 ft (4.5 m)
❄❄ ◐ ◌ ☼

### Trachycarpus wagnerianus

The miniature, evergreen Chusan palm has a vertical trunk with shiny, oval, rigid leaves slashed into splayed fingers. Bought as a young house plant, it will stay small for a long time. Stand it outside over summer, but bring under cover in winter.

**H**: 7½ ft (2.4 m), **S**: 30 in (75 cm)
❄❄ ◌ ☼

### Yucca gloriosa

The Spanish dagger, with its burst of swordlike leaves, is a shrub with great presence. It sends up late-summer flower spikes, packed with bunches of white flowers. 'Variegata' has yellow-edged leaves. Water moderately in summer, less in winter.

**H**: 4 ft (1.2 m), **S**: 4 ft (1.2 m)
❄❄ ◌ ☼

# Tall plants for shade (Ac–Ta)

### Acer palmatum
The deciduous Japanese maple has many cultivars, all grown for their spring leaves, attractive summer shape, and fall colors. Protect from cold winds and late frost. The slow-growing, mound-forming var. *dissectum* has finely divided leaves.

**H**: 4 ft (1.2 m), **S**: 6 ft (2 m)
❄❄❄ ◗ ◌ ◑ ☼

### Aucuba japonica
Evergreen spotted laurel makes a rounded shrub with shiny leaves and mid-spring reddish purple flowers; females carry red fall berries. Forms include self-fruiting 'Rozannie' and gold-splashed 'Variegata'. Water well and give liquid fertilizer in summer.

**H**: 6 ft (1.8 m), **S**: 6 ft (1.8 m)
❄❄❄ ◗ ◌ ◑

### Camellia japonica
Species and cultivars flower in early spring, in shades of red, pink, and white. A superb evergreen shrub for a large pot filled with ericaceous soil and given protection from cold winds and early morning sun. Prune lightly for shape after flowering.

**H**: to 6 ft (1.8 m), **S**: to 4 ft (1.2 m)
❄❄❄ ◗ ◌ ◑

### Camellia x williamsii
The advantage of x *williamsii* and its cultivars is that some flower in late winter, others in early and late spring. The color range is silver-white to deep pink. Compact pink 'Donation' starts flowering in late winter. See *C. japonica* for growing conditions.

**H**: to 6 ft (1.8 m), **S**: to 4 ft (1.2 m)
❄❄❄ ◗ ◌ ◑

### Eriobotrya japonica
Evergreen loquat is a great foliage shrub (or small tree) with striking, leathery leaves reaching up to 12 in (30 cm) long. After a long, hot summer it produces hawthornlike white flowers, opening in fall from woolly buds. Provide sun and shelter.

**H**: 6 ft (1.8 m), **S**: 6–10 ft (2–3 m)
❄❄ ◗ ◌ ◑ ☼

### Fargesia nitida
Fountain bamboo makes a tight clump of purple-green stems that arch gently. An open position is best; avoid deep shade. Use a straight-sided pot filled with a mix of soil, peat-based mix, and composted bark. Water well and fertilize in summer.

**H**: 10 ft (3 m), **S**: 3 ft (1 m)
❄❄❄ ◌ ◗ ◑

### x Fatshedera lizei
The tree ivy is a climbing evergreen shrub that needs a support. A cross between ivy and fatsia, its large, shiny, leathery leaves outclass the tiny greenish fall flowers. A good choice for a lightly shaded wall, but protect from severe weather.

**H**: to 6 ft (1.8 m), **S**: 3 ft (1 m)
❄❄ ◐ ○ ☼ ☼

### Hedychium densiflorum
One of the tallest perennial ginger lilies, it comes from the Himalayas and makes a real impact. It has long, glossy, pointed leaves and, at the end of summer, packed clusters of tiny orange or yellow flowers with a superb scent.

**H**: 12 ft (4 m), **S**: 4 ft (1.2 m)
❄❄ ◐ ○ ☼

### Holboellia coriacea
An exceptional, underrated evergreen climber, making strong growth with richly scented spring flowers (the males are mauve, the females greenish white). Provide a sheltered site in light shade or full sun, and wall wires to support the growth.

**H**: 11 ft (3.6 m)
❄❄ ◐ ○ ☼ ☼

### Kalmia latifolia
The calico bush is a dense shrub with shell-pink flowers opening from crimped buds, from late spring. The best forms include 'Freckles' with pink flowers and a spotted rim, and 'Pink Charm'. Grow in ericaceous soil; trim lightly after flowering for shape.

**H**: 5 ft (1.5 m), **S**: 5 ft (1.5 m)
❄❄❄ ◐ ○ ☼ ☼

### Osmanthus x burkwoodii
A top choice for the scented garden, this evergreen rounded shrub has a liberal covering of tubular white flowers in mid- and late spring. Shiny leathery leaves enliven the show all summer. Water well over summer, giving a monthly liquid fertilizer.

**H**: 5 ft (1.5 m), **S**: 5 ft (1.5 m)
❄❄❄ ◐ ○ ☼ ☼

### Taxus baccata
Good for topiary, evergreen yew can be cut into geometric forms. 'Standishii' is a good cultivar for a pot; at 4 ft (1.2 m) high and 24 in (60 cm) wide, it makes a golden yellow column. Trim for shape in late summer. Berries are produced on female plants.

**H**: 8 ft (2.5 m) **S**: 4 ft (1.2 m)
❄❄❄ ◐ ○ ☼ ☼

# Medium-sized plants for sun (Ab–Ch)

### Abutilon megapotamicum
A shrubby plant covered in little red and yellow flowers and fresh green leaves in summer. Train the main, gently arching stems against a wall or tie to canes. Bring under cover at the end of summer. Prune sideshoots by two-thirds in spring.

**H**: 36 in (90 cm), **S**: 36 in (90 cm)
❋❋ ◐ ◊ ☼

### Aeonium 'Zwartkop'
A striking, fashionable plant with shrubby stems topped by a rosette of deep dark purple, almost black leaves. Grow in cactus mix set off by a top layer of gravel. Water freely over summer, letting it dry out between drinks. Keep dry in winter.

**H**: to 36 in (90 cm), **S**: to 36 in (90 cm)
❋❋ ◊ ☼ ☀

### Agapanthus
The blue or white African lilies are best highlighted in Versailles tubs or ornamental pots; they hate heavy garden soil. Even the hardiest dislike the cold, and might not flower, so stick to the Headbourne Hybrids. Water well in summer; feed monthly.

**H**: to 30 in (75 cm), **S**: 18 in (45 cm)
Most ❋❋❋ ◊ ☼ ☀

### Aloe
An eye-catching succulent with yellow summer flowers on erect, branching spikes; the long, pointed fleshy leaves are gray-green. Stand outside in summer, then move under cover. Water moderately in summer, sparingly in winter; feed occasionally.

**H**: 24 in (60 cm), **S**: 24 in (60 cm)
❀ ◊ ☼

### Amaranthus caudatus
Theatrically called love-lies-bleeding because of the long, bright red flower tassels, this tropical annual makes a showy plant from midsummer into fall. Feed and water well. Sow seed in spring, and stand plants in a sheltered spot, tied to canes.

**H**: 36 in (90 cm), **S**: 36 in (90 cm)
❋ ◐ ◊ ☼

### Amaranthus tricolor
Chinese spinach makes a flamboyant, bushy foliage plant that is lipstick-red at its flashiest, with quieter kinds in green, often with added bronze, gold or pink tints. 'Joseph's Coat' is brash red and gold. Grow from seed sown in spring.

**H**: 36 in (90 cm), **S**: 12 in (30 cm)
❋ ◐ ◊ ☼

**Anthemis tinctoria** *'E. C. Buxton'*
The perennial golden marguerite gives a cottage-garden show with pale lemon yellow flowers in early summer. 'Beauty of Grallach' is orange-gold, 'Sauce Hollandaise' pale yellow. Cut back hard after flowering to force fresh growth from the base.

**H**: 24 in (60 cm), **S**: 24 in (60 cm)
❋❋ ◊ ☼

**Argyranthemum foeniculaceum**
An indispensable shrubby plant with white, daisylike flowers that quickly perk things up. Nip out the growing tips in spring for a bushier shape, and deadhead to encourage a succession of flower buds. Bring under cover in fall; cut back hard next spring.

**H**: to 36 in (90 cm), **S**: 24 in (60 cm)
❋ ◑ ◊ ☼

**Artemisia** *'Powis Castle'*
With its dense, silvery mound of feathery leaves, this is a good "contrast plant" used with stronger, bolder colors, or as part of a gentle pastel scheme. Give it a hard spring pruning after shoots start appearing at the base of the woody stem.

**H**: 24 in (60 cm), **S**: 36 in (90 cm)
❋❋ ◑ ◊ ☼

**Astilbe** *'Fanal'*
'Fanal' has dark red flowers in early summer and dark green leaves. Alternatives include 'Purpurlanze', with purple-red late summer flowers; lilac-pink 'Hyazinth', and white 'Irrlicht', which blooms in late spring. Keep the soil moist in summer.

**H**: 24 in (60 cm), **S**: 18 in (45 cm)
❋❋❋ ◑ ☼

**Canna**
Cannas make strong focal points. 'Wyoming' has brown-purple leaves with purple veins, 'Durban' has green- and pink-striped foliage; both have orange flowers. Cut off top-growth when frost comes; store the rhizomes in a frost-free place.

**H**: to 5 ft (1.5 m), **S**: to 18 in (45 cm)
❋ ◑ ◊ ☼

**Chamaecyparis pisifera** *'Nana'*
A mini-mound of a conifer, ideal for use in a trough, with sprays of light green foliage with a dash of silver beneath. Alternatives include yellow-speckled 'Plumosa Aurea' and 'Nana Aureovariegata', and 'Silver Lode' with white flecking at the leaf tips.

**H**: 30 in (75 cm), **S**: 24 in (60 cm)
❋❋❋ ◑ ◊ ☼

# Medium-sized plants for sun (Cl–Fu)

### Cleome hassleriana
A small clump of the annual spider plant is eye-catching in a large container. The upright, scented petals come in a range of colors (white, pink, lilac, and purple), but note the vicious spines at the junction of leaf and stem. Raise from seed.

**H**: 36 in (90 cm), **S**: 16 in (40 cm)
❀ ◐ ◊ ☀

### Convolvulus cneorum
A compact shrub that performs all summer, with yellow-centered white flowers opening from pink buds, set against silver-green foliage. Use well-drained, gritty potting mix. Stand in full sun but give shelter in winter. Lightly prune for shape after flowering.

**H**: 18 in (45 cm), **S**: 24 in (60 cm)
❄ ❄ ◊ ☀

### Cosmos atrosanguineus
Chocolate cosmos is well worth growing for its unusual, deep maroon flowers on top of long, thin stems held well clear of the foliage. On hot, sunny days, they smell like chocolate. Bring under cover over winter, and water it occasionally.

**H**: 24 in (60 cm), **S**: 18 in (45 cm)
❄ ❄ ◐ ◊ ☀

### Cosmos bipinnatus
A colorful annual, easily grown from seed in spring, with white, pink, or red flowers on top of stems with filigree leaves. Selections include the compact Sonata Series and 'Sea Shells', which has unusual rolled-up petals. Deadhead for more flowers.

**H**: to 36 in (90 cm), **S**: to 18 in (45 cm)
❄ ◐ ◊ ☀

### Chrysanthemum carinatum 'Court Jesters'
Easily grown from seed, this annual produces an open-rayed flower, usually white or yellow with a hint of red around the purple eye. Fast-growing and quick-branching, it creates a summer-long show.

**H**: 18 in (45 cm), **S**: 9 in (23 cm)
❄ ◐ ◊ ☀

### Dahlia 'Bishop of Llandaff'
Highly rated, with scarlet flowers and black-red foliage. When leaves are blackened by frost (or in mid-fall), slice off stems at the base and stand tubers upside down for three weeks in an airy, frost-free place. Store over winter in bark chips.

**H**: 30 in (75 cm), **S**: 18 in (45 cm)
❄ ◐ ◊ ☀

**Dahlia *'Hayley Jane'***
A bicolor in white with purple-pink edges, ideal for pastel schemes or to brighten up stronger colors. Insert strong canes in the soil when planting in spring. Growing dahlias in pots helps stop slugs from savaging new growth. See *D.* 'Bishop of Llandaff'.

**H**: 36 in (90 cm), **S**: 24 in (60 cm)
❄ ◐ ◌ ☼

**Dahlia *'Hillcrest Royal'***
This rich purple dahlia has a strong presence. Nip out the main growing tip after four weeks to promote bushier growth and more flowers; keep deadheading. Give a tomato fertilizer from midsummer to promote new buds. See *D.* 'Bishop of Llandaff'.

**H**: 30 in (75 cm), **S**: 18 in (45 cm)
❄ ◐ ◌ ☼

**Dahlia *'Moonfire'***
A useful small dahlia that gets off to a quick start, with rich yellow flowers and bronze leaves. Grow it in front of taller, more richly colored dahlias, or use to encircle a large barrel featuring more dominant plants. See *D.* 'Bishop of Llandaff' for growing tips.

**H**: 24 in (60 cm), **S**: 12 in (30 cm)
❄ ◐ ◌ ☼

**Euonymus alatus *'Compactus'***
This dwarf, dense form of the deciduous winged spindle has dark green foliage that flares deep red in fall. The branches are corky; pale red fruit follows insignificant light green summer flowers. Do not let the shrub bake dry in summer.

**H**: 30 in (75 cm), **S**: 30 in (75 cm)
❄❄❄ ◐ ◌ ☼ ◔

**Festuca glauca**
With its porcupine spines in silver blue, the evergreen grass blue fescue adds a distinctive note to any scheme, especially those with strong sculptural forms. There are spikelets of flowers in early and midsummer. Bright blue 'Blaufuchs' is an excellent cultivar.

**H**: to 12 in (30 cm), **S**: 10 in (25 cm)
❄❄❄ ◌ ☼

**Fuchsia *'Checkerboard'***
Often grown as a standard, this striking, elegant fuchsia has red and white flowers. Replacement buds appear all summer, when it will need regular fertilizing. Cut back in spring to promote new growth. Bring under cover in winter and keep just moist.

**H**: 30 in (75 cm), **S**: 18 in (45 cm)
❄ ◐ ◌ ☼

# Medium-sized plants for sun (Fu–Sk)

### Fuchsia 'Thalia'

A non-blowzy fuchsia, 'Thalia' has thin red tubular flowers set against olive green, red-veined leaves. It has a vigorous, upright shape, but nip out the stem tips in late spring to make it bushier. Fertilize through summer; bring under cover in fall.

**H**: to 30 in (75 cm), **S**: to 30 in (75 cm)

### Grindelia chiloensis

A summer-flowering shrub (evergreen in mild winters), with cornflower-like yellow flowers, held on stout, single stems, well clear of the bushy growth and gray-green leaves. It needs plenty of sun and well-drained soil. Cut off any frost-damaged parts.

**H**: 30 in (75 cm), **S**: 30 in (75 cm)

### Hebe vernicosa

A small rounded evergreen shrub from New Zealand with shiny, dark green leaves. Slender spikes of white flowers (which might initially be pale lilac) appear at the start of summer. Give a gentle pruning if required, to smarten it up after flowering.

**H**: 24 in (60 cm), **S**: 36 in (90 cm)

### Hydrangea macrophylla

Common hydrangeas (*H. macrophylla*) have two forms: mopheads, with rounded flower clusters, and lacecaps, with flattened heads. Acidic soil forces lilac flowers; alkaline promotes pink (whites stay white). Grow in a sheltered position.

**H**: to 5 ft (1.5 m), **S**: to 6 ft (1.8 m)

### Lavandula

Shrubby, scented lavender attracts butterflies and bees. *L. angustifolia* has gray-green leaves, 'Hidcote' is more silvery with purple flowers, while 'Loddon Pink' is pale pink. French lavender, *L. stoechas*, has dark purple petals like rabbit's ears.

**H**: to 3 ft (1 m), **S**: to 3 ft (1 m)

### Nicotiana alata

A tobacco plant grown for its pink, greenish yellow, white, and purple summer flowers with evening scent. It has large, distinctive leaves. Give it a prominent position as it comes into flower, and grow from seed every year in spring.

**H**: to 36 in (90 cm), **S**: 12 in (30 cm)

### Philadelphus 'Belle Etoile'

One of the best-scented midsummer shrubs, with a rich aroma of vanilla and bubblegum. Give it a sunny, sheltered spot and a large pot for plenty of root and top growth. Water freely in summer; fertilize monthly. Prune to a new bud after flowering.

**H**: 36 in (90 cm), **S**: to 6 ft (1.8 m)
❄❄❄ ◗ ◊ ☼ ◑

### Phormium 'Sundowner'

Grown for its striking shape, 'Sundowner' has stiffly upright, bronze-green leaves with pinkish edges: a good choice in architectural schemes. Yellow-green flowers appear in summer, high above the foliage. Well-drained soil is vital.

**H**: 36 in (90 cm), **S**: 36 in (90 cm)
❄❄ ◗ ◊ ☼

### Platycladus orientalis 'Aurea Nana'

A rounded mini-conifer with flat sprays of light yellow-green leaves in winter, followed by much brighter yellowish new leaves in spring, which hold their color well until fall. A good architectural pot plant.

**H**: 36 in (90 cm), **S**: 36 in (90 cm)
❄❄❄ ◗ ◊ ☼

### Rosa x odorata 'Mutabilis'

A beautiful shrubby rose with a mass of pinkish red new stems and leaves in spring, followed by summer-long flower clusters. Flowers open buff-yellow, turning pink and pale crimson before falling, giving a mixed tapestry. Prune by half in late winter.

**H**: 36 in (90 cm), **S**: 36 in (90 cm)
❄❄ ◗ ◊ ☼

### Salvia x sylvestris

One of a trio of salvias—with S. x superba and S. nemorosa—that make extremely attractive rounded bushes. Spikes poke up above the foliage with clustered, pale blue flowers with a hint of pink through early summer. 'Rose Queen' is soft pink.

**H**: 24 in (60 cm), **S**: 9 in (23 cm)
❄❄❄ ◗ ◊ ☼

### Skimmia japonica 'Rubella'

It stands out in winter with its clusters of tiny, reddish brown buds—set above dark green leaves—on red stalks. White flowers open from mid-spring, and females will have berries if you plant this male close to them. Trim lightly for shape after flowering.

**H**: 4 ft (1.2 m), **S**: 4 ft (1.2 m)
❄❄❄ ◗ ◊ ☼ ◑

# Medium-sized plants for shade (As–He)

### Asplenium scolopendrium
A shapely evergreen for shade, hart's-tongue fern makes a bright green show of leathery, shiny fronds. Good cultivars include Crispum Group, with wavy margins, and Cristatum Group, crested at each frond's tip. Give half-strength liquid fertilizer in summer.

**H**: 24 in (60 cm), **S**: 24 in (60 cm)
❄❄❄ ◊ ◊ ☼

### Begonia 'Dragon Wing'
This annual has prolific red flowers that hang down in summer until stopped by frost (pink and white forms are now also available). It is ideal for hanging baskets, with lush growth spreading out over the sides. Water well and fertilize over summer.

**H**: 12 in (30 cm), **S**: 14 in (35 cm)
❄ ◊ ◊ ☼ ☼

### Berberis thunbergii 'Atropurpurea Nana'
A small, purple bushy mound of a deciduous shrub—the dwarf form of f. atropurpurea—that really stands out in fall when the foliage "burns" eye-catching red before falling. A good patio plant in a four-season display.

**H**: 24 in (60 cm), **S**: 28 in (75 cm)
❄❄❄ ◊ ◊ ☼ ☼

### Buxus sempervirens 'Suffruticosa'
Common boxwood is an evergreen shrub with dense growth and small leaves, widely used for topiary. Trim to shape in both early and late summer, by eye or using frames. Fertilize over summer.

**H**: to 4 ft (1.2 m), **S**: to 3 ft (1 m)
❄❄❄ ◊ ◊ ☼

### Carex flagellifera
A New Zealand perennial with dense growth, it has long, bronze, arching leaves and beige flower spikes in summer. Makes an effective contrast at the foot of bright green verticals, such as Crocosmia 'Lucifer'. Easy, but avoid overwatering and drought.

**H**: 36 in (90 cm), **S**: 36 in (90 cm)
❄❄ ◊ ◊ ☼ ☼

### Danae racemosa
Shrubby Alexandrian laurel sends up slender, bamboolike shoots in spring. The foliage is the attraction, the tiny whitish flowers amounting to little, though the red berries are a bonus. Cut back old shoots in early spring. Divide in fall for new plants.

**H**: 30 in (75 cm), **S**: 30 in (75 cm)
❄❄ ◊ ◊ ◊ ☼ ☼

## Daphne laureola

Not as richly scented as some daphnes, but the evergreen spring laurel is still worth growing for its glossy, dark green leaves and tiny, clustered yellow-green flowers in late winter and early spring. They are followed by black fruit.

**H**: 28 in (75 cm), **S**: 4 ft (1.2 m)
❄❄❄ ◐ ◊ ◑ ☼

## Daphne mezereum

A scented, deciduous shrub for late winter and early spring. Pink-purple flowers appear on bare wood; f. *alba* is white. Underplant with spring bulbs to take over as flowers fade. Provide shelter to preserve its exquisite scent; do not let the soil bake dry.

**H**: 36 in (90 cm), **S**: 36 in (90 cm)
❄❄❄ ◐ ◊ ◑ ☼

## Dryopteris filix-mas

The easy-to-grow male fern is more than a gap-filler. Its new, fresh green fronds poke out of the ground and start uncoiling in spring, bearing divided fronds and rust-brown scales; it turns dull green in summer. Cut back to soil level in early winter.

**H**: 30 in (75 cm), **S**: 30 in (75 cm)
❄❄❄ ◐ ◊ ◑

## Euphorbia amygdaloides *var.* robbiae

A bushy, evergreen perennial, wood spurge has lime green flowers in spring, turning dark green in summer and eventually coral red. Plants seed into cracks in paving and walls. Cut off stems at the base after flowering.

**H**: 30 in (75 cm), **S**: 12 in (30 cm)
❄❄❄ ◐ ◊ ◑ ☼

## Hedera helix

Evergreen ivy can be incredibly vigorous, so you need a restrained form for a trellis or a hanging basket. Frost-hardy 'Duckfoot' has light green leaves; 'Goldchild' gray-green foliage with yellow edging; 'Parsley Crested' bright green, crinkle-edged leaves.

**H**: to 6 ft (2 m)
❄❄ ◐ ◊ ◑ ☼

## Helleborus orientalis

The perennial Lenten rose is meant to peak in spring but often blooms in midwinter with open, saucerlike flowers. Colors range from greenish white to pinkish purple, mauve and deep purple; the best are speckled. White *H. niger* flowers in midwinter.

**H**: to 24 in (60 cm), **S**: to 24 in (60 cm)
❄❄❄ ◐ ◊ ◑

# Medium-sized plants for shade (Ho–Vi)

### Hosta 'Francee'
A showy perennial with puckered green leaves, white-splashed around the edges, and pale blue summer flowers. Offset it with gravel-topped soil. 'Frosted Jade' is also green with white edging. Keep well watered; avoid flaying winds.

**H**: 20 in (50 cm), **S**: 3 ft (1 m)
❄❄❄ ◐ ◊ ☼

### Hosta sieboldiana *var.* elegans
The rounded, gray-blue leaves stand out clearly, being puckered or channeled with a ripple effect. This is a good choice for shade. Provide a sheltered spot for the container and make sure the soil stays well watered in hot, dry spells.

**H**: 30 in (75 cm), **S**: 3 ft (1 m)
❄❄❄ ◐ ◊ ☼

### Hydrangea serrata '*Bluebird*'
A deciduous, upright shrub, *H. serrata* has flat-topped flowerheads. 'Bluebird' is one of the best of many cultivars. It has a long summer-to-fall show of blue flowers; the leaves redden in fall. Prune one-third of stems to the base in spring.

**H**: 30 in (75 cm), **S**: 36 in (90 cm)
❄❄ ◐ ◊ ☼ ☼

### Ligularia dentata '*Desdemona*'
This lush perennial has large, purple-reddish young leaves that turn green on top, and spires of orange flowers in midsummer. Try standing it near a water feature. Keep the soil moist in summer, and shelter from strong winds. Beware of slugs.

**H**: 3 ft (1 m), **S**: 3 ft (1 m)
❄❄❄ ◐ ◊ ☼

### Lonicera fragrantissima
A bushy evergreen widely grown for its scented, creamy white flowers at the end of winter. Stand against a protective wall. Cut back to a strong bud after flowering, and entirely remove one-quarter of the old stems to soil level.

**H**: 36 in (90 cm), **S**: 36 in (90 cm)
❄❄ ◊ ◐ ☼ ☼

### Lunaria annua
The annual honesty has late-spring and summer flowers, from white to purple; 'Variegata' is eye-catching, with its green and white leaves. Both have paper-thin, semitranslucent seedheads, excellent in cut-flower arrangements. Sow seed in spring.

**H**: 30 in (75 cm), **S**: 9 in (23 cm)
❄❄❄ ◐ ◊ ☼ ☼

### Pieris japonica '*Little Heath*'

The leaves of this dwarf form of the evergreen species initially have a pink tinge but later stand out because of their attractive white edging. White flowers open in late winter and spring. Use ericaceous potting mix, and stand in a sheltered position.

**H**: 24 in (60 cm), **S**: 24 in (60 cm)
❄❄❄ ◔ ◌ ◑ ☼

### Polygonatum x hybridum

Solomon's seal is a superb perennial that flowers in spring, when a row of green-tipped, white flowers dangle along the arching green stems. 'Striatum' has creamy white striped leaves. Provide woodland-like conditions with damp shade.

**H**: to 4 ft (1.2 m), **S**: 12 in (30 cm)
❄❄❄ ◔ ◌ ◑ ☼

### Polystichum

The best holly ferns include *P. aculeatum*, which thrives in deep shade. Its narrow, shiny, dark green fronds form a shuttlecock shape. The soft shield fern, *P. setiferum*, can be twice the size. Remove old fronds as new ones unfurl in spring.

**H**: to 3 ft (1 m), **S**: to 36 in (90 cm)
❄❄❄ ◔ ◌ ◑

### Rudbeckia hirta '*Kelvedon Star*'

An eye-catching version of black-eyed Susan, with a dark mahogany brown slash up the base of the bright yellow petals, which are set around a dark central eye, making 4-in- (10-cm-) wide flowers. Essential for the second half of summer into fall.

**H**: 36 in (90 cm), **S**: 36 in (90 cm)
❄❄❄ ◔ ◌ ◑ ☼

### Ruscus aculeatus

The shrubby, evergreen butcher's broom perks things up in fall when females bear masses of bright red, poisonous berries. They follow on from tiny, inconspicuous flowers and stand out against the dark green "leaves." A good plant for dry shade.

**H**: 30 in (75 cm), **S**: to 3 ft (1 m)
❄❄❄ ◔ ◌ ◑ ☼

### Viburnum davidii

One of the smaller viburnums, this makes compact, dense, evergreen mounding growth packed with shiny, dark green leaves. The late-spring, dull white flowers are followed by bluish berries (if you have a male and female), which stand out in winter.

**H**: 36 in (90 cm), **S**: 36 in (90 cm)
❄❄❄ ◔ ◌ ◑ ☼

# Short plants for sun (Bi–Gy)

### Bidens ferulifolia
A short-lived perennial with open, starlike, bright yellow flowers at the ends of thin, wiry stems from summer to fall. Often grown in hanging baskets to snake through adjacent plants. 'Golden Goddess' has finer leaves and larger flowers.

**H**: to 12 in (30 cm), **S**: 36 in (90 cm)
❄❄ ◊ ○ ☀

### Brassica oleracea
Ornamental cabbages were bred for their leafy colors, bright and brash in reds, pinks, purples, and white. The colors intensify with colder fall temperatures. Use them in rows of pots, to front a container display. Grow from seed in spring.

**H**: to 18 in (45 cm), **S**: to 18 in (45 cm)
❄❄❄ ◊ ○ ☀

### Campanula isophylla
Use the perennial Italian bellflower in hanging baskets: its trailing stems, with starlike blue flowers, dangle effectively over the sides. Contrast it with white 'Alba' or 'Stella White'. Feed, but do not overwater, in summer. Bring under cover in winter.

**H**: 8 in (20 cm), **S**: 18 in (45 cm)
❄ ◊ ☀ ☼

### Capsicum annuum
There are two kinds of ornamental peppers: the large, fleshy kind for roasting or using raw in salads, and the thinner, hotter kind for Asian cooking. Both are available in a wide color range. Sow seed in late winter, and grow in a sunny, sheltered site.

**H**: to 30 in (75 cm), **S**: 12 in (30 cm)
❀◊ ○ ☀

### Carex elata 'Aurea'
Bowles' golden sedge is a graceful, deciduous perennial that makes an effective clump of slender, arching yellow leaves with green stripes. Do not let the soil bake dry over summer, and stand where the sun highlights its color.

**H**: 24 in (60 cm), **S**: 12 in (30 cm)
❄❄❄ ◊ ○ ☀ ☼

### Crocus
Flowering after hyacinths and before tulips, crocuses can front large pots filled with evergreen shrubs. The late winter/early spring C. chrysanthus varieties include 'Blue Pearl' (pale blue with a yellow throat) and lemon yellow 'E. A. Bowles'.

**H**: 3 in (7 cm), **S**: 2 in (5 cm)
❄❄❄ ◊ ○ ☀

### Dianthus
Perennial pinks are ideal for stone troughs or old sinks. Old-fashioned kinds give the best scent, in particular the white, ragged-edged 'Mrs. Sinkins' and 'Brympton Red'. Dead-head for a long summer show; use sandy potting mix for good drainage.

**H**: to 12 in (30 cm), **S**: to 12 in (30 cm)
❀❀❀ ◐ ◊ ☼

### Echeveria elegans
An evergreen succulent with a rosette of thick, fleshy leaves, often with a powdery bloom, and tall flower spikes. *E. elegans* has pink flowers, orange inside. Stand several pots outside in front of a large container, but bring indoors for winter.

**H**: 2 in (5 cm), **S**: 2 in (5 cm)
❀ ◐ ◊ ☼

### Felicia amelloides
A blue-flowering shrubby daisy that flowers all summer; bring under cover in winter. Popular forms include the rich blue 'Santa Anita' (also with variegated leaves), 'Read's Blue' and 'Read's White'. Fertilize in summer, but water sparingly in winter.

**H**: 24 in (60 cm), **S**: 24 in (60 cm)
❀ ◐ ◊ ☼

### Festuca glauca 'Blaufuchs'
The blue fescue is a clump-forming evergreen grass with late-spring flower spikes. Good cultivars include the silver-blue 'Blue Fox' ('Blaufuchs') and 'Elijah Blue'; 'Seeigel' is bluish green. Divide every two years to maintain fresh young plants.

**H**: 12 in (30 cm), **S**: 12 in (30 cm)
❀❀❀ ◊ ☼

### Gaillardia x grandiflora 'Kobold'
A brash, fun annual with an outer ring of yellow around the red petals, and a dark red center. Pack in at the front of large tubs that need a color boost. Grow from seed in spring, and deadhead to maintain the supply of new flower buds.

**H**: 24 in (60 cm), **S**: 12 in (30 cm)
❀❀❀ ◐ ◊ ☼ ◑

### Gypsophila repens
Ideal for stone troughs, this pretty little perennial makes a mat of semi-evergreen growth with bursts of tiny, star-shaped, white or pink flowers in summer. 'Dorothy Teacher' is shorter, with bluish green leaves and dark pink flowers. Good drainage is vital.

**H**: 8 in (20 cm), **S**: 12 in (30 cm)
❀❀❀ ◊ ☼

# Short plants for sun (He–Na)

### Helichrysum petiolare
A tender, shrubby perennial, often grown as an annual for its trailing, branching stems and rounded, silver, woolly leaves. Keep the soil dry over winter. Place it where the stems can snake through adjacent plants.

**H**: 16 in (40 cm), **S**: 5 ft (1.5 m) when trailing
❄ ◐ ◌ ☼

### Heliotropium arborescens
The small, shrubby cherry pie gives a superb vanilla scent. The flowers are purple-blue ('Chatsworth'), violet (e.g., 'Lord Roberts'), or white ('White Lady'). Fertilize monthly in summer; bring under cover for winter and keep just moist. Renew by cuttings.

**H**: to 18 in (45 cm), **S**: to 18 in (45 cm)
❄ ◐ ◌ ☼ ◑

### Hordeum jubatum
The annual or short-lived perennial squirrel tail grass gives a relaxed show with its long, silvery plumes, often tinged purple at the tip. Use several around the perimeter of a large tub with taller, architectural plants within. Grow from seed sown in spring.

**H**: 10 in (25 cm), **S**: 3 in (8 cm)
❄❄❄ ◐ ◌ ☼

### Hyacinthus orientalis
The waxy, petal-packed hyacinth spikes come in white, blue, pink, red, and yellow, with a rich scent on warm, still days in mid- and late spring. Plant in front of a summer-flowering shrub, or with spring bedding. Excellent in window boxes.

**H**: 8 in (20 cm), **S**: 12 in (30 cm)
❄❄❄ ◌ ☼

### Lagurus ovatus
The annual, tufted hare's tail grass has fluffy flowerheads, which can be picked for drying before they have matured, and pale green leaves. Sow seed in spring, or in cold frames in fall. 'Nanus' is a mini version, 5 in (12 cm) high.

**H**: 18 in (45 cm), **S**: 10 in (25 cm)
❄❄❄ ◌ ☼

### Lobelia erinus
The species has numerous trailing forms, all easily grown from seed in spring. Cascade Series, ideal for hanging baskets, has a mass of flowering stems in white, blue, and red. Regatta Series flowers early; 'Rosamund' is red with a white eye.

**H**: 6 in (15 cm), **S**: 4 in (10 cm)
❄ ◌ ◐ ☼

### Lotus berthelotii

Parrot's beak is an exotic, shrubby trailer ideal for hanging baskets. It has a mix of black-centered, yellow-orange to scarlet flowers like lobster's claws, and needlelike, silver-gray leaves. Grow it outside over summer, and water and fertilize regularly.

**H**: 8 in (20 cm), **S**: 36 in (90 cm)
❄ ◊ ☼

### Mammillaria bombycina

Visit a specialist nursery for the best choice of pincushion cacti; most are small, globular, and flower prolifically. *M. bombycina* has hooked spines poking through white down, creating a showy clump in summer; *M. pringlei* has red flowers.

**H**: 12 in (30 cm), **S**: 12 in (30 cm) or more
❀ ◊ ☼

### Mentha

Being a rampant spreader, mint is often best grown in a pot of its own. You won't go wrong if you stick to spearmint (*M. spicata*) and applemint (*M. suaveolens*). Bring under cover in winter and you will get early shoots next spring. Repot every few years.

**H**: 30 in (75 cm), **S**: Indefinite
❄❄❄ ◊ ☼

### Muscari armeniacum

The grape hyacinth bulb makes a gentle spring show. It has short spikes barnacled with tiny blue flowers, and grasslike foliage. When clumps get congested, lift from the soil during summer dormancy and gently separate; replant 4 in (10 cm) deep.

**H**: 8 in (20 cm), **S**: 3 in (8 cm)
❄❄❄ ◊ ◗ ☼

### Narcissus

The daffodil season kicks off with the rich yellow *N. bulbocodium*, then *N.* 'Rijnveld's Early Sensation' and 'February Gold', and ending with *N. poeticus* var. *recurvus*. Remove dying flowerheads, but let the foliage die down naturally.

**H**: to 18 in (45 cm), **S**: to 6 in (16 cm)
❄❄❄ ◊ ◗ ☼

### Narcissus 'Minnow'

A quick-multiplying Tazetta daffodil for mid-spring. Its flowers have soft yellow cups that gradually fade to off-white, and are surrounded by a ray of six creamy "petals." A good choice at the sunny base of a shrub in a wooden tub.

**H**: 7 in (18 cm), **S**: 4 in (10 cm)
❄❄❄ ◊ ☼

# Short plants for sun (Oc–Sa)

### Ocimum basilicum
Some seed catalogs offer about 20 different kinds of basil, mostly green but some reddish. 'Purple Ruffles' has large, purple, curled leaves; 'Dark Opal' is red-purple. One of the best culinary greens is 'Napolitano'. Bring pots indoors in early fall.

**H**: to 18 in (45 cm), **S**: 12 in (30 cm)
❉ ◊ ◖ ☼

### Ophiopogon planiscapus 'Nigrescens'
An evergreen that looks like a black grass, lilyturf makes a small clump of straplike leaves, with sprays of mauvish white flowers in summer. Plant at the front of a display. Water freely and fertilize monthly in summer.

**H**: 8 in (20 cm), **S**: 12 in (30 cm)
❉❉❉ ◖ ◊ ☼ ◐

### Osteospermum
Perennials flowering from late spring to fall, needing sun to open the petals. Typically white, pink, or pale yellow, they add a cottage-garden touch; 'Whirligig' has mini teaspoon-like petals. Bring under cover in winter, and reduce watering.

**H**: to 18 in (45 cm), **S**: to 18 in (45 cm)
❉❉ ◊ ☼

### Pelargonium 'Century Hot Pink'
Grown for its lipstick pink flowers, and well worth mixing with the other reds, pinks, and white in the Century Series. Nip back any straggly growth just above a shoot to create a bushier, more flowery plant. A good ingredient for a mix of summer annuals.

**H**: 18 in (45 cm), **S**: 12 in (30 cm)
⌂ ◖ ◊ ☼

### Pelargonium 'Clorinda'
A shrubby pelargonium with stiff stems and clusters of lovely soft pink flowers in summer. The lobed leaves are mildly scented. Summer cuttings root quickly: take as replacements when older plants become leggy and bare. Move under cover in winter.

**H**: 24 in (60 cm), **S**: 24 in (60 cm)
⌂ ◖ ◊ ☼

### Petroselinum crispum
Both the ornamental curled and the stronger tasting flat-leaf parsley are best grown in large pots to prevent slugs from attacking young plants. Sow seed in plug trays or small pots in early spring—parsley hates being disturbed. Do not let the soil dry out.

**H**: 18 in (45 cm), **S**: 10 in (25 cm)
❉❉❉ ◖ ◊ ☼

### Petunia

Versatile annuals for every container from baskets to tubs, petunias give a long, reliable show of summer color. There are punchy reds and blues, as well as pinks, pale yellow, and white. Water well over summer, giving a semi-weekly high-potash fertilizer.

**H**: to 10 in (25 cm), **S**: to 36 in (90 cm)
❄ ◊ ☼

### Picea abies *'Little Gem'*

This Christmas tree relative, with its flattish dome of light green leaves, is an instant hit. It can be grown in troughs or old sinks and looks good in spring, covered in bright green new growth. It is slow-growing, taking 10 years to reach 12 in (30 cm).

**H**: 12 in (30 cm), **S**: 36 in (90 cm)
❄❄❄ ◊ ☼

### Potentilla *'Gibson's Scarlet'*

A brash little perennial grown for its early to late-summer scarlet flowers, which are nicely set against the green foliage. Best grown at the front of a large container. It will grow happily in poor soil mixed with plenty of sand for fast drainage.

**H**: to 18 in (45 cm), **S**: 24 in (60 cm)
❄❄❄ ◊ ☼

### Rosa *'Snowball'*

A miniature rose, introduced in 1984, with a mass of white flowers, each as big as a thumbnail, which appear all through the summer. Cut back stems by half in early spring, and fertilize well over summer. At its best, it really does look like a large snowball.

**H**: 8 in (20 cm), **S**: 8 in (20 cm)
❄❄ ◊ ◊ ☼

### Salvia patens

The flowers of this rich blue perennial have an open mouth; 'Cambridge Blue' is paler. It fits a range of color schemes, and looks good with the maroon *Cosmos atrosanguineus* and yellow *Bidens ferulifolia*. Protect over winter; take spring cuttings.

**H**: 24 in (60 cm), **S**: 24 in (60 cm)
❄❄ ◊ ◊ ☼

### Saxifraga

Shallow-rooting, mainly alpine plants, most making spreading, ground-hugging growth, with rosettes of tactile, overlapping leaves. The spring flowers tend to be in the white-pink-lemon range. 'Tumbling Waters' has silver-green leaves and white flowers.

**H**: 18 in (45 cm), **S**: 12 in (30 cm)
❄❄❄ ◊ ☼

# Short plants for sun (Sc–Vi)

### Scabiosa atropurpurea
### *'Chile Black'*
The pincushion has small, dark red flowers (verging on black) with white specks, which will leap out of a pastel group or perk up a hot color scheme. It is a short-lived perennial, but spring cuttings take quickly.

**H**: 24 in (60 cm), **S**: 9 in (23 cm)
✽✽✽ ◐ ◊ ☼

### Sedum
Two of the best stonecrops are the mat-forming kind (*S. spathulifolium*), with tiny leaf rosettes and yellow flowers, ideal for alpine troughs, and the taller, deciduous perennials (*S.* 'Herbstfreude') with pink summer flowers. Add sand to the soil.

**H**: 4 in (10 cm), **S**: to 30 in (75 cm)
✽✽✽ ◊ ☼

### Sempervivum
Perennial houseleeks make shapely rosettes of pointed, fleshy leaves, the most striking in mahogany and reddish shades. After the summer sprays of star-shaped flowers, the rosettes die but are replaced by new growth. Grow in alpine troughs.

**H**: 6 in (15 cm), **S**: to 18 in (45 cm)
✽✽✽ ◊ ☼

### Senecio pulcher
Best grown in pots to avoid winter weather, it has red-purple flowers in early fall. Most leaves, roughly oval-shaped at the base, and lancelike on the stem, hang on over winter. Water moderately in summer, with the occasional drink in winter.

**H**: 18 in (45 cm), **S**: 18 in (45 cm)
✽✽ ◊ ☼

### Solenostemon
Grow coleus for the flamboyant leaves, which range from black to yellow with red speckles. Many are annuals, but named ones, like *S.* 'Display', are short-lived perennials. Pinch out early growth, and give high-nitrogen fertilizer semiweekly.

**H**: to 24 in (60 cm), **S**: to 24 in (60 cm)
❀◐ ◊ ☼

### Tagetes
Small, easy-to-grow French marigolds come in mahogany, orange, and yellow, and have a long flowering season. The Signet Gem series includes 'Lemon Gem', 'Little Gem' and 'Tangerine Gem'. Sow seed in spring and keep deadheading.

**H**: 12–16 in (30–40 cm), **S**: 12 in (30 cm)
✽ ◐ ◊ ☼

**Thymus**
Evergreen thymes offer contrasting shapes and leaf color. Tiny-leaved *T. herba-barona* spreads across the soil surface, while forms of *T. vulgaris* can be snipped into mounds; 'Silver Posie' has gray/silver markings. Well-drained soil is vital; trim often.

**H**: to 12 in (30 cm), **S**: to 18 in (45 cm)
Most ❄❄❄ ◗ ◊ ☼

**Tropaeolum** *(trailing)*
Grow trailing nasturtiums so that their stems scramble through adjoining plants and spill out of hanging baskets. The vigorous annual *T. majus* has orange, red, and yellow flowers; the perennial *T. speciosum* is bright red.

**H**: to 12 in (30 cm), **S**: to 11 ft (3.5 m)
❀ ◗ ◊ ☼

**Tulipa 'China Pink'**
The flowers are an exquisite shade of satin pink, fading to a white blotch in the center of the cup, giving an elegant, long-lasting, late spring show. An old favorite (raised in 1944) that is still a big seller. Use in formal, stately schemes.

**H**: 20 in (50 cm)
❄❄❄ ◗ ◊ ☼

**Tulipa 'Flaming Parrot'**
A fun, eccentric showoff for late spring, with strong feathered red lines against a creamy yellow background. Try grouping it with multicolored tulips like the red and white 'Estella Rijnveld' and 'Carnaval de Nice' for a lively, pantomime mix.

**H**: 22 in (55 cm)
❄❄❄ ◗ ◊ ☼

**Verbena 'Sissinghurst'**
This pink-flowered perennial can be theatrically trained up a pyramid of short canes wrapped with string, or planted with silver-leaved plants. Grow it in hanging baskets to dangle over and down the sides. Water freely in full growth; fertilize monthly.

**H**: to 8 in (20 cm), **S**: to 18 in (45 cm)
❄❄ ◗ ◊ ☼

**Viola**
Hardy pansies have a huge color range, many with striking markings, others intricately beautiful. Some flower in winter/early spring (a sunny spot is vital), and others in late spring and summer. Most are annuals. Keep deadheading regularly.

**H**: to 10 in (25 cm), **S**: to 12 in (30 cm)
❄❄❄ ◗ ◊ ☼

# Short plants for shade (Ad–Er)

### Adiantum venustum
The evergreen maidenhair fern is grown for its mix of thin, black stems and new bronze-pink fronds, which gradually turn fresh green. The rhizomes need space to spread; it makes an effective miniature for the front of a scheme.

**H**: 6 in (15 cm), **S**: to 12 in (30 cm)
❄❄❄ ◍ ○ ◐ ☀

### Alchemilla mollis
Lady's mantle is a good space filler: it has pale green leaves that hold drops of rain, and sprays of greenish yellow flowers. A prolific self-seeder, it scatters new plants freely. Shear after flowering to stop this, and encourage fresh, new growth.

**H**: 16 in (40 cm), **S**: 16 in (40 cm)
❄❄❄ ◍ ○ ◐ ☀

### Arum italicum
A high-scoring perennial for its striking, pale green, early-summer spathe surrounding a creamy white spadix, followed by orange-red, toxic berries. It has large, white-veined leaves; those of 'Marmoratum' are showier, marbled with pale green.

**H**: 12 in (30 cm), **S**: 6 in (15 cm)
❄❄❄ ◍ ○ ◐ ☀

### Begonia pendula
Flowering prolifically from early summer to the first frosts, it comes in red, pink, orange, yellow, and white. Plant the tubers 1 in (2.5 cm) deep, ideally in a hanging basket because of its spreading growth, and water well in dry spells. Feed regularly.

**H**: 12 in (30 cm), **S**: 18 in (45 cm)
❄ ◍ ○ ◐ ☀

### Bergenia
Elephant's ears has large, glossy evergreen leaves and white, pink or red flowers in spring. Magenta-flowered *B. cordifolia* 'Purpurea' has large leaves that redden up in winter; *B. purpurascens* turns beet red. Avoid direct sun.

**H**: to 18 in (45 cm), **S**: to 18 in (45 cm)
❄❄❄ ◍ ○ ◐

### Carex buchananii
An evergreen sedge with slender, arching, copper-bronze leafy growth; best grown against a light background. There are brown flower spikes in mid- and late summer. Do not let it dry out in warm spells, but avoid waterlogging.

**H**: 24 in (60 cm), **S**: 30 in (75 cm)
❄❄ ◍ ◐ ☀

## Convallaria majalis

Lily-of-the-valley is one of the best plants for light shade, with its white, sweetly scented flowers set against shapely leaves. 'Albostriata' is eye-catching because of its white-striped leaves; 'Hardwick Hall' has creamy to yellow-edged leaves.

**H**: 9 in (23 cm), **S**: 12 in (30 cm)
❄❄❄ ◊ ☼ ☼

## Corydalis flexuosa

A woodland perennial producing a mass of feathery, light green leaves and blue tubular flowers from late spring to summer. There are several cultivars: bright blue 'Père David', and deep blue 'China Blue' and 'Purple Leaf'. Grow it with yellow *C. lutea*.

**H**: to 12 in (30 cm), **S**: to 12 in (30 cm)
❄❄❄ ◊ ◊ ☼

## Cuphea '*Tiny Mice*'

With red and purple flowers said to look like a mouse's ears, this blooms from summer to the first frosts. Keep pinching out new growth to increase the plant's bushiness, and water and feed well in summer. It reportedly attracts hummingbirds.

**H**: 8 in (20 cm), **S**: 12 in (30 cm)
❄ ◊ ☼ ☼

## Cyclamen coum

A tuberous perennial with white, pink, or red flowers from late winter to spring. The leaves range from dark green to silver-patterned. Pewter Group varieties have leaves that are almost silver on top. Use gritty soil with leaf mold; plant shallowly.

**H**: 2½ in (6 cm), **S**: 4 in (10 cm)
❄❄❄ ◊ ☼

## Epimedium *x* rubrum

A quiet, low-key perennial, its new, pointed leaves have a reddish tinge in spring and again in winter before falling. Dull red or pale yellow flowers with short spurs appear in the second half of spring. Give it a position sheltered from cold winds.

**H**: 9 in (23 cm), **S**: 9 in (23 cm)
❄❄❄ ◊ ◊ ☼

## Erythronium

The spring-flowering dog's-tooth violets are beautiful small perennials. Typically the flowers are white, pink, yellow, purple, and violet; many have distinctive, mottled foliage. Keep the soil damp, especially over a long, hot summer.

**H**: 9 in (23 cm), **S**: 9 in (23 cm)
❄❄❄ ◊ ◊ ☼

# hort plants for shade (Eu–Tr)

### Euonymus fortunei
An evergreen shrub with some first-rate cultivars. Best for a container is 'Emerald 'n' Gold', with yellow-edged green leaves turning reddish in winter (a degree of sun aids the variegation). The more dwarf 'Emerald Cushion' has a mound of lush green leaves.

**H**: 24 in (60 cm), **S**: 24 in (60 cm)
❄❄❄ ◊♦ ☼ ☼

### Fuchsia 'Tom Thumb'
A dwarf, upright, bushy fuchsia, as popular now as when raised in France in 1850. The flower tube at the top is red, with flared red wings and a mauve skirt beneath. It starts flowering early in summer, and never lets up until fall.

**H**: 9 in (23 cm), **S**: 9 in (23 cm)
❄❄ ◊ ◊ ☼ ☼

### Gaultheria procumbens
The checkerberry makes low, spreading growth with shiny, dark green leaves and white or pale pink flowers in summer, followed by rich red berries through winter. If transferring to the open garden, use as groundcover in acidic soil.

**H**: 6 in (15 cm), **S**: to 3 ft (1 m)
❄❄ ◊ ☼

### Hakonechloa macra 'Aureola'
A perennial grass that makes a vivid mound of bright yellow leaves with a few slender, green stripes. In deep shade, the variegation is lime green, and in cool conditions it tends to be creamy white. Makes a good contrast with rounded and upright shapes.

**H**: 12 in (30 cm), **S**: 12 in (30 cm)
❄❄❄ ◊◊ ☼ ☼

### Heuchera micrantha var. diversifolia 'Palace Purple'
A prized container perennial because of its shiny, bronze-purple, jagged leaves, highlighted by early summer sprays of tiny, greenish white flowers. Avoid shade. Replant in early fall with the crown above the soil.

**H**: 18 in (45 cm), **S**: 18 in (45 cm)
❄❄❄ ◊♦ ☼ ☼

### Impatiens
Busy Lizzies are incredibly popular and there are many excellent hybrids like the New Guinea group and cultivars of *I. walleriana*. *I. niamniamensis* 'Congo Cockatoo' has flashy red and yellow hooded flowers. Many impatiens thrive in shade.

**H**: to 20 in (50 cm), **S**: to 24 in (60 cm)
❄◊ ☼ ☼

### Isotoma axillaris

Usually grown as an annual for its long spring-to-fall show of open, starlike flowers on slender, branching stems. The blooms range from pale to deep blue, occasionally white. Do not overwater, fertilize once a month, and keep deadheading.

**H**: 12 in (30 cm), **S**: 12 in (30 cm)

### Lamium maculatum

A clump-forming perennial with triangular, dark green leaves, and pinkish purple late spring to summer flowers. Its spreading growth creates a groundcover effect in a large pot. 'White Nancy' has tiny silver leaves with a green rim and white flowers.

**H**: 9 in (23 cm), **S**: 9 in (23 cm)

### Liriope muscari

Lilyturf is a woodland plant, with tiny violet-mauve fall flowers held on a spike, and straplike dark green leaves. 'John Burch' has gold-variegated leaves; 'Monroe White' needs full shade. Provide ericaceous potting mix and shelter from cold winds.

**H**: 9 in (23 cm), **S**: 12 in (30 cm)

### Polygonatum hookeri

A short, creeping form of Solomon's seal with late-spring/early summer star-shaped flowers, from pale to deep pink, followed by black fruit. It makes an intriguing little pot plant for a shady corner; cover the top of the soil with gravel.

**H**: 4 in (10 cm), **S**: 12 in (30 cm)

### Primula Wanda Supreme Series

Perennials with bronze to dark green leaves and a cheery show of flowers in shades of blue, yellow, purple, pink, and red, from winter to mid-spring. Plants like moist, rich soil; seed can be sown in early spring. The primrose (*P. vulgaris*) flowers until late spring.

**H**: 3 in (8 cm), **S**: 6 in (15 cm)

### Tricyrtis formosana

The toad lily is an exquisite perennial with upright to arching stems, and upward-facing fall flowers. They come in quiet colors—mauves, yellows, and cream—often with a mass of tiny spots. Slugs and snails attack new growth.

**H**: to 30 in (75 cm), **S**: to 18 in (45 cm)

# Index

# Index

Japanese maple *see Acer*
*Jasminum*
  *J. officinale* 127
  *J. polyanthum* 119
*Juniperus communis*
  *J. c.* 'Brynhyfryd Gold' 127
  *J. c.* 'Compressa' 127

## K, L

*Kalmia latifolia* (calico bush) 133
kettles 104
kitchen garden basket 86–7
*Kniphofia* (red hot poker) 100
labeling 61
ladders for containers 102
lady's mantle *see Alchemilla mollis*
*Lagurus ovatus* (hare's-tail grass) 146
  *L. o.* 'Nanus' 146
*Lamium maculatum* 155
  *L. m.* 'Aureum' 82
  *L. m.* 'White Nancy' 155
*Lantana camara* 119, 127
*Lathyrus odoratus* (sweet pea) 128
laurel *see Aucuba; Danae racemosa*
*Laurus nobilis* (bay) 24, 100, 128
*Lavandula* (lavender) 13, 93, 104, 138
  *L. angustifolia* 138
    *L. a.* 'Hidcote' 138
    *L. a.* 'Loddon Pink' 138
  *L. stoechas* 15, 138
lavender *see Lavandula*
leaf fertilizer 111
leaf miners 115
lemon tree 125
Lenten rose *see Helleborus orientalis*
lettuce 'Lollo Rosso' 86
*Leucanthemum vulgare* 19
*Ligularia dentata* 'Desdemona' 142
*Lilium* (lily)
  *L.* Citronella Group 128
  *L. regale* 13, 15, 128
    *L. r.* 'Album' 128
lily *see Agapanthus; Hedychium; Lilium; Tricyrtis*
lily beetles 115
lily-of-the-valley *see Convallaria majalis*
lilyturf *see Liriope; Ophiopogon*
lime-hating plants, feeding 111
*Liriope muscari* (lilyturf) 155

*L. m.* 'John Burch' 155
*L. m.* 'Monroe White' 155
*Livistonia chinensis* (Chinese fan palm) 119, 128
loam-based potting mix 44
*Lobelia* 19, 74
  *L. erinus* 146
  *L. e.* Cascade Series 146
  *L. e.* Regatta Series 146
  pruning 113
*Lobelia cardinalis* 128
*Lonicera* (honeysuckle) 16
  *L. fragrantissima* 142
loquat *see Eriobotrya japonica*
*Lotus berthelotii* (coral gem) 22, 147
love-lies-bleeding *see Amaranthus caudatus*
*Lunaria annua* (honesty) 142
  *L. a.* 'Variegata' 142

## M

*Mahonia*, pruning 113
maidenhair fern *see Adiantum venustum*
*Mammillaria bombycina* 147
maple, Japanese *see Acer*
marguerites *see Leucanthemum vulgare*
  perennial *see Anthemis tinctoria*
marigold, French *see Tagetes*
*Mattheuccia struthopteris* 100
Mediterranean planting 20–1, 94–7
medium-sized plants
  for shade 140–3
  for sunny sites 134–9
*Melianthus major* (honeybush) 78, 129
*Mentha* (mint) 20, 147
  *M. spicata* 147
  *M. suaveolens* 147
metal balls 34
metal containers 13, 37
  rust prevention 38
Mexican orange blossom *see Choisya ternata*
mint *see Mentha*
*Miscanthus* 97
montbretia *see Crocosmia*
morning glory *see Ipomoea*
mountain flax *see Phormium*
mulches 48–9
  for climbers 59
  for shrubs 53
*Musa basjoo* (banana plant) 101
  protection 119

*Muscari* (grape hyacinth)
  *M. armeniacum* 147
  *M. neglectum* 66
*Myrrhis odorata* (sweet Cicely) 15
*Myrtus communis* subsp. *tarentina* (myrtle) 129

## N

*Narcissus* (daffodil)
  dwarf 23
  *N. bulbocodium* 147
  *N.* 'February Gold' 147
  *N.* 'Jetfire' 68
  *N.* 'Minnow' 147
  *N. poeticus* var. *recurvus* 147
  *N.* 'Rijnveld's Early Sensation' 147
nasturtium *see Tropaeolum*
*Nemesia* 105
*Nerium oleander* (rose bay) 119, 129
  *N. o.* 'Casablanca' 129
  *N. o.* 'Ruby Lace' 129
New Zealand cabbage palm *see Cordyline australis*
New Zealand flax *see Phormium tenax*
*Nicotiana alata* (tobacco plant) 138
*Nolina recurvata* 129

## O

*Ocimum basilicum* (basil) 20, 148
*Olea europaea* (olive) 129
olive *see Olea europaea*
*Ophiopogon planiscapus* 'Nigrescens' (lilyturf) 148
orange scheme 32
oregano *see Origanum vulgare*
*Origanum vulgare* (oregano) 20
*Osmanthus* x *burkwoodii* 133
*Osteospermum* 35, 148
  *O.* 'Whirligig' 148
overwintering plants 118–19

## P

palms 19, 98, 101, 128, 129
pansy *see Viola*
parsley *see Petroselinum*
*Passiflora caerulea* (blue passionflower) 129
passionflower *see Passiflora*

patios 8–25
  designing 28–9
  themed effect 88–105
pavers 29
peat-based potting mix 44
peat-free potting mix 45
pebble mulch 49
*Pelargonium* 10, 19, 105
  *P.* 'Century Hot Pink' 148
  *P.* 'Clorinda' 97, 148
  protection 119
pepper, ornamental *see Capsicum*
perfume
  contemporary planting 13
  spring planting 66–7
  summer planting 15
pergola 94–5
pests 43, 114–15
*Petroselinum* (parsley) 20
  *P. crispum* 148
*Petunia* 23, 92, 96, 100, 105, 149
*Philadelphus* 'Belle Etoile' 139
*Phormium* (mountain flax) 13, 97
  *P.* 'Sundowner' 101, 139
  *P. tenax* 130
    *P. t.* 'Dazzler' 130
*Phyllostachys nigra* (black bamboo) 13
*Picea abies* 'Little Gem' 149
picture framing 20
*Pieris* 100
  *P. japonica* 'Little Heath' 143
  pruning 113
pillars 19
pink scheme 23, 35, 76–7
pinks *see Dianthus*
planting
  combinations 32–3, 66–87
  shrubs 49–53
plants, choosing for health 42–3
plastic containers 37
*Platycladus orientalis* 'Aurea Nana' 139
*Plectranthus madagascariensis* 70
*Polygonatum* (Solomon's seal)
  *P. hookeri* 155
  *P.* x *hybridum* 143
*Polystichum*
  *P. aculeatum* 143
  *P. setiferum* 143
*Potentilla* 'Gibson's Scarlet' 149
potting mix 44–5
powdery mildew 117
*Primula* 9, 23
  *P. vulgaris* 68, 155
  *P.* 'Wanda' 80
  *P.* Wanda Supreme Series 155
pruning 112–13

# Acknowledgments

The publisher would like to thank the following for their kind permission to reproduce their photographs:

(Key: a-above; b-below/bottom; c-center; l-left; r-right; t-top)

**8:** Modeste Herwig: Hampton Cottage. **9:** The Garden Collection: Marie O'Hara (bl). John Glover: (br). **10:** The Garden Collection: Gary Rogers/Designers: Monika Johannes & Malte Droege-Jung. **11:** John Glover: Designer: Alan Titchmarsh (t), Liz Eddison/RHS Chelsea Flower Show 2005/Designers: Geoff & Josh Whiten (bl), The Garden Collection: Liz Eddison (br). **12:** Derek St Romaine: Hampton Court Flower Show 2000/ Designer: Susanna Brown. **13:** Garden Picture Library: Linda Burgess (t),Leigh Clapp: Hampton Court Flower Show. Designer Susan Slater (br), The Garden Collection: Liz Eddison/Hampton Court Flower Show 2000/Designers: Wynniatt-Husey Clarke (bl). **14:** The Garden Collection: Gary Rogers/Hampton Court Flower Show 2005/Designer: Hadrian Whittle (t), The Garden Collection: Liz Eddison/RHS Chelsea Flower Show 2002/ Designer: Miriam Book (br). Garden Picture Library: John Glover (bl). **15:** The Garden Collection: Liz Eddison/RHS Chelsea Flower Show 2003/Designer: Michelle Brown. **16:** Harpur Garden Library: Designer: Luciano Giubbilei, London. **17:** Andrew Lawson: The Old Rectory, Sudborough (tc). Derek St Romaine: (tr), Mrs Penny Snell (tl), Mrs Jenny Raworth (b). **18:** The Garden Collection: Liz Eddison/Designers: Lloyd Christie. **19:** The Garden Collection: Marie O'Hara (t); Derek St Romaine/Designers: Mr & Mrs Jolley, Maycotts, Kent (br). John Glover: Designer: Jonathan Baillie (bl). **20:** The Garden Collection: Liz Eddison/

RHS Chelsea Flower Show/Designer: Geoff Whiten (t). Derek St Romaine: RHS Chelsea Flower Show 2003. The Goldfish Garden. Designer Geoff Whiten (b). **21:** Garden Picture Library: Linda Burgess. **22:** The Garden Collection: Liz Eddison (tl) (tr), Janet Johnson: (bl), Andrew Lawson: (br), **23:** S & O Mathews Photography: Morrinsville, NZ. **24:** Leigh Clapp: (t). John Glover: York Gate, Leeds (b). **25:** DK Images: Steve Wooster/RHS Chelsea Flower Show/Designers: Lloyd Christie (t). Andrew Lawson. RHS Chelsea Flower Show 1996. Designer Stephen Woodhams (b). **26–27:** DK Images: Steve Wooster/ Bulbeck Foundrey. **28:** Derek St Romaine: Designer: Phil Nash for Mr Gary Holden. **29:** John Glover: RHS Chelsea Flower Show 1997/Woking Borough Council (tr), The Garden Collection: Liz Eddison/ Designers: Rob Jones, Matthew Stewart & Ben Gluslowski (br). **30:** Derek St Romaine: (t). **31:** Harpur Garden Library: Chanticleer (t). **32:** DK Images: Steve Wooster/RHS Chelsea Flower Show 2002/ A Moveable Modular Garden/Designer: Natalie Charles. **33:** Harpur Garden Library: Designer: Christopher Bradley-Hole, London (br). **34:** Andrew Lawson: RHS Chelsea Flower Show 2002 (tl), Leigh Clapp: The Little Cottage (tr), The Garden Collection: Derek St Romaine/Designers: Anthony Tuite and Grainne Farren (br). **37:** DK Images: Steve Wooster/RHS Chelsea Flower Show 2002/A Moveable Modular Garden/Designer: Natalie Charles (b). **48:** John Glover: RHS Chelsea Flower show 1997/Woking Borough Council. **66:** Derek St Romaine: (bl). **67:** Derek St Romaine. **69:** Andrew Lawson: Whichford Pottery. **79:** DK Images: Mark Winwood/ Hampton Court Flower Show 2005, Designer S J Granger: Centrifugal Chic. **87:** John Glover. **88–89:** Derek St Romaine: Hampton Court Flower Show

2000/Designer: Susanna Brown. **90:** Brian T. North. **90–91:** Brian T. North. **92:** Brian T. North: (t) (bl) (br). **94:** Brian T. North: (bl). **94–95:** Brian T. North. **96:** Brian T. North: (t) (bl) (br). **97:** Brian T. North: (t) (bl) (br). **98–99:** Derek St Romaine: Mr & Mrs Bates. **100:** Andrew Lawson: (br). **102–103:** Brian T. North. **104:** Garden Picture Library: Linda Burgess (t). Brian T. North: (bl) (br). **105:** Leigh Clapp: Hampton Court Flower Show/Designer: Sheila Fishwide (bl). Brian T. North: (br). **111:** The Garden Collection: Derek St Romaine/Designers: Mr & Mrs P Hickman, Little Lodge (b). **114:** Holt Studios International: Michael Mayer/FLPA (tr). **115:** RHS Tim Sandall (tr) and (cl), Holt Studios International: Nigel Cattlin/FLPA (c). **117:** Science Photo Library: Geoff Kidd (bc). **122–123:** DK Images: Steve Wooster/ RHS Chelsea Flower Show 2002/ Designer: Natalie Charles. **124:** Garden World Images: (br). **125:** crocus.co.uk (tr). **127:** Garden World Images: (tr). **129:** Garden World Images: (bl). **139:** crocus. co.uk (tl), Garden World Images: (bl). **140:** Garden World Images: (br). **143:** Garden World Images: (bl). **145:** Garden World Images: (tr). **149:** Garden World Images: (tc)

All other images © Dorling Kindersley For further information, see: www.dkimages.com

**Dorling Kindersley would also like to thank the following:**
*Editors for Airedale Publishing*: Helen Ridge, Fiona Wild, Mandy Lebentz *Designers for Airedale Publishing*: Elly King, Murdo Culver *Index*: Michèle Clarke